Foundations of Modern Economics Series

Otto Eckstein, *Editor*

AMERICAN INDUSTRY:
STRUCTURE, CONDUCT, PERFORMANCE
Richard Caves

PRICE THEORY
Robert Dorfman

MONEY AND CREDIT: IMPACT AND CONTROL
James S. Duesenberry

LABOR ECONOMICS
John T. Dunlop

PUBLIC FINANCE
Otto Eckstein

ECONOMIC DEVELOPMENT: PAST AND PRESENT
Richard T. Gill

ECONOMIC SYSTEMS
Gregory Grossman

INTERNATIONAL ECONOMICS
Peter B. Kenen

NATIONAL INCOME ANALYSIS
Charles L. Schultze

PRENTICE-HALL, INC., ENGLEWOOD CLIFFS, NEW JERSEY

FOUNDATIONS OF MODERN ECONOMICS SERIES

Peter B. Kenen

Columbia University

INTERNATIONAL
ECONOMICS

PRENTICE-HALL
FOUNDATIONS OF MODERN ECONOMICS SERIES

Otto Eckstein, *Editor*

HF
1411
.K4
(2)

PRENTICE-HALL INTERNATIONAL, INC., *London*
PRENTICE-HALL OF AUSTRALIA, PTY. LTD., *Sydney*
PRENTICE-HALL OF CANADA, LTD., *Toronto*
PRENTICE-HALL FRANCE, S. A. R. L., *Paris*
PRENTICE-HALL OF INDIA, PVT. LTD., *New Delhi*
PRENTICE-HALL OF JAPAN, INC., *Tokyo*
PRENTICE-HALL DE MEXICO, S. A., *Mexico City*

FOUNDATIONS
OF MODERN ECONOMICS SERIES

Economics has grown so rapidly in recent years that no one book can present it authoritatively today. *Foundations of Modern Economics* is a series of concise books surveying the major branches of the discipline, each written by a leading economist in the midst of the research and discussion of his specialty. Taken individually, each book reflects the structure, the content and the key scientific and policy issues of its field. The Series as a whole presents an account of Economics designed to be the material for the basic one-year college course.

v

Two of the nine books present the analytical core of Economics, *Price Theory* and *National Income Analysis*. Study of one or both of the core books is recommended before entering into the various fields of application. *Economic Development: Past and Present,* which uses a more historical approach, can be read without prerequisite and can serve as an introduction.

This new approach, as compared to the usual textbook, has several advantages. By mirroring the actual state of knowledge and discussion, the books gain in interest, depth, and relevance. They also communicate some of the excitement of the current research in a developing field.

The books free the teacher to devise his own course curriculum, rather than to follow the format of the textbook. Any selection or order of topics is possible once analytical principles have been mastered. Specific areas can be explored at greater length. The teacher not interested in a complete survey course can eliminate several of the books, spending more time on detailed study of a few fields. One-semester courses, emphasizing only micro-economics, or only macro-economics, can also be readily devised.

The books do not offer settled conclusions. They show the student the central problems of each field, and show how economic analysis permits more intelligent thinking about them. The Series is offered in the hope that this firsthand exposure will equip the student better as a citizen, and will attract him to the further pursuit of the subject.

Otto Eckstein, *Editor*

CONTENTS

2

Trade and Resource Allocation, 7

3

Problems in Trade Policy, 31

4

The Balance of Payments and Foreign-Exchange Market, 51

5

International Financial Policy, 77

6

Toward an International Economy, 97

THE NATION AS AN ECONOMIC UNIT

Foreign and Domestic Transactions

International economics is among the oldest specialties within economic inquiry. It was conceived in the sixteenth century, a lusty child of Europe's passion for Spanish gold, and was born two centuries later, with Adam Smith attending. The child soon turned against its parents—the pamphleteers and politicians who had sought to extract gold from other countries' coffers by restricting imports and expanding exports—and instead supported free trade in Britain's press and Parliament. In the nineteenth century, it attracted some of the very best economists, whose work on foreign trade and payments left us a valuable legacy. John Stuart Mill, for example, gave us the first full formulation of "the law of supply and demand" while explaining price determination in international markets. A large part of monetary theory emerged from early efforts to show how foreign trade can affect the domestic price level.

The subject flourishes today because the facts that brought it into being still compel attention. First, economic conditions and institutions are more uniform within countries than they are between countries. Second, foreign transactions are specially encumbered by public policy.

Language, law, and custom rarely differ much within a single country. This internal uniformity makes for easy movement of men, money, and enterprise. Tax and monetary systems are also homogeneous within a country, but differ very markedly from one country to the next. True, the tax systems of our 50 separate states vary widely. But federal tax rates are higher than state rates, and you may deduct state-tax payments from your gross income to calculate your federal income tax. The national tax system thereby helps to average out regional differences. Furthermore, federal spending tends to overlay and offset local variations in the quality and quantity of public services.

Internal monetary differences are very slight. An elaborate market network connects financial institutions within the United States. Funds can flow from one region to the next, keeping credit conditions closely aligned. Borrowers can raise cash where it is cheapest, whittling down regional differences. Finally and most important, a single currency is used all over the country. A five-dollar bill issued by the Federal Reserve Bank of Richmond circulates freely throughout the United States; it must be accepted everywhere. For that matter, you can cash a check wherever you are known, even if you write the check on a bank several hundred miles away. How much more complicated life would be if merchants would not accept currency or checks from other Federal Reserve Districts! You would have to scan every dollar bill, weed out those from other Districts, and swap them for local money at a bank; you would also have to carry considerable cash while traveling and would have to trade one kind for another when crossing state lines.

Goods flow freely between our 50 states. In fact, the American Constitution expressly forbids local interference with interstate commerce. The authors of the Constitution rightly believed that free trade among the states would help cement their fragile union. Today, France, Italy, Germany, the Netherlands, Belgium, and Luxembourg are forging a Common Market in Western Europe as their first step toward confederation; they will soon permit a free flow of goods inside Western Europe and will impose a common tariff on goods from outside. But trade between countries is ordinarily burdened with national tariffs which work to raise the prices of imported goods; and trade may sometimes encounter absolute barriers—quotas that restrict the quantity of imports or a person's freedom to buy and use foreign currency. The United States places quotas on foreign petroleum and on each of a dozen farm products. Quotas on imported oil protect the domestic oil industry. Quotas on farm products reserve to American farmers the benefits provided by our high farm price supports. Tariffs and quantitative import barriers are doubly restrictive. First, they raise the prices of foreign goods and handicap those goods in competition with domestic products. Second, they impose a heavy workload on the would-be importer. Look at the fragment from the U.S. tariff schedule reproduced as Fig. 1, and try to compute the rate of duty on a shockproof, self-winding watch with 16 jewels.

PARA. 367(a)(1-5): Watches and watch movements, and timekeeping, measuring or indicating mechanisms, devices, and instruments, whether or not designed to be worn or carried on or about the person, less than $1^{77}/_{100}$ inches wide, whether or not in cases, etc., with or without dials.

Having more than 15, but not more than 17 jewels:

More than $1\frac{1}{2}$, less than $1^{77}/_{100}$ inches wide	$1.25	ea.
More than $1^2/_{10}$, not more than $1\frac{1}{2}$ inches wide	1.35	ea.
More than 1, not more than $1^2/_{10}$ inches wide	1.35	ea.
More than $^9/_{10}$, not more than 1 inch wide	1.75	ea.
More than $^8/_{10}$, not more than $^9/_{10}$ inches wide	2.00	ea.
More than $^6/_{10}$, not more than $^8/_{10}$ inches wide	$2.02\frac{1}{2}$	ea.
$^6/_{10}$ inches, or less wide	2.50	ea.

Adjustments and jewels in movements having more than 15, but not more than 12 jewels:

Adjustments (adjustment to temperature equals 2 adjustments)	.50	ea. add'l
Jewels	$.13\frac{1}{2}$	ea. add'l
Movements operating in excess of 47 hours without rewinding or if self-winding	.75	ea. add'l

FIG. 1 A fragment from the U.S. Tariff Schedule. The tariff on a single watch must be calculated by adding up several separate rates: the basic rate (based on width and jewels), the extra duty on adjustments, the duty on each jewel, and the special duty on self-winding mechanisms.

Differences between monetary policies may have an even greater impact than tariffs and quotas. Almost all international transactions involve two or more moneys. An American wholesaler importing French champagne has first to determine the price of the wine in French francs, then the price of the franc in dollars—the franc-dollar *exchange rate*. He must order the champagne, buy French francs with dollars, then transfer the francs to the French exporter. He will thereby incur extra costs and run extra risks. The costs are the commissions charged by foreign-exchange dealers. The risks arise because exchange rates can change. Most governments are pledged to maintain the exchange rates at or near fixed figures called parities. Currently, for example, you can buy a French franc for 20¼ cents, or $4^{47}/_{50}$ French francs for a dollar. But governments allow the exchange rates to change by as much as 2 per cent of parity in response to variations of supply and demand, and sometimes change the parities themselves. In 1956 the French franc was *devalued* (became cheaper in terms of other currencies), going from 3½ for a dollar to 4⅕ for a dollar; and in 1958 it was devalued again, this time from 4⅕ to $4^{47}/_{50}$. In 1961, by contrast, the German mark and the Dutch guilder were made to *appreciate* (became dearer in terms of other currencies). Day-to-day changes in exchange rates can cut into traders' profits, and sudden changes in parities can turn profits into losses. The importer of champagne could lose heavily if the price of the franc were to rise on the foreign-exchange market after he had signed his sales contract but before he had bought his francs.[1]

The foreign investor must also cope with foreign-exchange problems, and these may be much more complex than those the trader faces. The investor has a longer time-horizon. He will also face some tricky tax problems, as tax laws and tax rates differ radically from one country to the next.

The international economist looks at the world as a community of separate nations, each with its own constellation of natural resources, capital, knowledge, and manpower, its own social and economic institutions, and its own economic policies. He usually assumes that domestic transport costs are negligible and that domestic markets are purely competitive. He often assumes that labor and capital are perfectly mobile within every country, but not free to move from one country to the next.

Using these assumptions, he seeks to explain flows of foreign trade and foreign investment, to assess their impact on domestic welfare, and to forecast their response to changes in policy. He concentrates on policies designed to affect foreign trade and payments—those involving tariffs, exchange rates, and the taxation of foreign-source income. But he also looks at domestic policies—tax rates, public spending, monetary management, labor legislation, and antitrust laws—since they prescribe the terms on which foreign trade takes place.

Perspectives and Criteria

The specialist in international economics will sometimes look at trade and payments from one country's standpoint, but he is just as likely to

[1] Traders and investors can protect themselves against exchange-rate changes by buying or selling foreign currency on the *forward* foreign-exchange market. There, they can arrange to swap dollars for francs three months from now, but at the price (exchange rate) fixed today. This way, however, they merely transform extra risks into extra costs, for forward foreign exchange may be more expensive than spot (current) foreign exchange.

adopt a cosmopolitan perspective. He may study trade and payments for their impact on the world as a whole. Taking the viewpoint of a single country, he is apt to start by pretending that the country has always been isolated from the outside world, then begins to trade with other countries. Taking the view of the world as a whole, he may start by pretending that the world was one country, then was carved up into separate territories, each with unique institutions and policies. It is very important to identify the author's perspective and starting point when you examine any work on foreign trade and payments.

Whatever his perspective, the international economist has a deep concern for the individual. Like other economists, he is an intellectual descendant of Adam Smith and of the nineteenth-century Utilitarians. Hence, he may treat the nation as a single unit, but not as the end in view. He will appraise a change in public policy by the same test as his colleagues in public finance or in labor economics. He will say that a change in policy is a good thing if those individuals who gain by the change could compensate those who lose. Furthermore, he uses the same tests of economic performance as other specialists:

First, he is concerned with *efficiency:* How do foreign trade and payments affect the allocation of resources within a country? How do they redistribute economic tasks among the participating countries?

Second, he is concerned with *equity:* How does trade alter the distribution of income and wealth within a country? How does it redistribute income among countries?

Third, he is concerned with *stability:* How does trade affect an economy's reaction to domestic disturbances? Does a country import extra instability through its foreign transactions? And do its international transactions affect its freedom to deal with domestic problems?

Fourth, he is concerned with *economic growth:* Does a country's foreign trade affect its growth rate? Should the less-developed countries gear their new production to foreign markets, making their way as exporters, or should they draw back from foreign trade, seeking greater self-sufficiency?

Do not be deceived by the abstract way in which I pose these questions. The search for answers is propelled by the daily needs of business and government, not by scientific curiosity alone. The problems posed by foreign trade, foreign investment, foreign aid, and by the international monetary system impinge on important problems of national policy. The United States must face a host of issues because its supply of raw materials is dwindling after a century of intensive exploitation. Should it cut back its domestic output of ores and oil, relying instead on cheaper foreign sources, or should it protect its domestic producers against import competition, encouraging domestic exploration and exploitation? What can this country do to improve the distribution of global food supplies? Can one reconcile the farm policies of key exporters like the United States and Canada with those of key importers like

Britain and India? Should tax policies be changed to respond to the surge of private American investment abroad—the building of plants in Europe to produce or assemble goods that were formerly exported by the United States? How will this migration of capital and enterprise affect income and employment at home and abroad?

How can the United States maintain equilibrium in its international transactions, given its commitment to combat domestic unemployment and to defend and develop friendly foreign countries? Is the special position of the dollar as an international currency beneficial or burdensome? If burdensome, how can the international monetary system be altered without damaging the network of trade and payments built so patiently since the Second World War? How best can the United States aid the new nations of Asia, Africa, and Latin America? How will these younger countries fit into world trade once they have begun to modernize their own economies?

I shall not be able to examine all these issues in a hundred pages, but can give you a taste of the methods and perspective which identify the international economist as he wanders through these problems. In Chapters 2 and 3, you will look at foreign trade and foreign investment as they affect resource allocation and economic welfare; you will glance at the diplomacy of trade policy and take a quick tour of the European Common Market. In Chapters 4 and 5, you will study the *balance of payments* and foreign-exchange market; you will look at equilibrium, displacement, and adjustment in international payments, then look at the roles of gold and the U.S. dollar as international currencies. Finally, in Chapter 6, you will examine foreign trade and foreign investment as "engines" of economic growth, and survey the ways they can foster the development of the new countries.

2

TRADE AND RESOURCE ALLOCATION

The Basis for Trade and Gains from Trade

Differences in prices are the basic cause of trade and reflect international differences in costs. But why should costs differ from country to country? How can Japan produce cameras, sewing machines, and cotton shirts more cheaply than the United States? Many people would reply that Japan has lower costs because it has lower wages, and wages are important costs. This familiar

7

explanation seems plausible enough; it is firmly based in fact. But it is not an adequate explanation.

If wage rates were decisive for costs and trade, low wage rates would allow Japan to undersell every foreign manufacturer and flood world markets with Japanese products. This could not go on for very long. Foreigners could not continue buying from Japan if they could not sell their products in Japan's own market and foreign governments would act to redress the balance. Furthermore, the demand for Japanese exports would rebound against Japan's economy. The demand for labor would exceed the supply, and Japanese wage rates would start to rise, raising Japan's costs and prices. Alternatively, the demand for these same goods would show up as a demand for Japanese currency. If, then, the exchange rates were free to fluctuate, the price of the yen would start to rise, raising the prices of Japanese products in foreign markets. Eventually, the prices of some Japanese products would exceed the corresponding foreign prices, and Japan would begin to import those products, though still exporting others. The Japanese price level (or Japanese exchange rate) would stabilize when Japan's sales on the world market were about equal to its purchases from other countries.

Briefly, a general difference in cost levels is not a sustainable basis for trade. An enduring pattern of trade and payments must be traced to differences in cost *structure* from country to country. Some things must be cheaper to produce at home and will be exported; others must be cheaper to produce abroad and will be imported. This generalization is sometimes called the *Principle of Comparative Advantage*. It asserts that countries will export the products they can make at lowest *relative* cost. Japan will export cameras and textiles because it can produce these goods at less cost compared to other goods than the United States or other industrial countries. The United States will export wheat and lathes because it can produce them at less cost compared to other goods. Cameras may be cheaper than lathes in both countries, but the cost difference is wider in Japan than in the United States. To explain a country's foreign trade, one must identify its comparative advantage, looking at its natural resources and man-made stock of skill and machinery.

NATURAL RESOURCES

Nature has decreed important and enduring differences between countries. One country is rich in copper, another in petroleum. One has a waterfall, another has a fertile plain. Some countries have adequate rainfall for rice or cotton, some have too much, others next to none.

Furthermore, some countries have combinations of natural resources eminently suited to certain economic tasks. One may have the plains *and* rainfall required to grow wheat. One may have a rich iron-ore deposit beside a major waterway that can carry ore to coal. Finally, some countries have populations large enough to support great, complex industries. Others are so underpopulated that land cannot be worked or ores extracted.

MAN-MADE RESOURCES

In one sense, people are a natural resource; in another, they are a precious man-made resource. Mere numbers are the gift of nature. But the skills and attitudes of the population are the work of man and strongly influence comparative advantage. A nation rich in manpower but poor in skill may be suited to certain tasks, but not to the production and export of manufactured goods. A nation that has very few people per square mile, but that has lavished its energies on technical education, is likely to enjoy a comparative advantage in the production of precision goods.

Going one step further, we must distinguish types of skill: Some nations have large numbers of factory workers adept at handling modern machinery. Others have an abundance of engineers and scientists and specialize in new, research-laden products. It has been said, for example, that the United States enjoys a comparative advantage in research and innovation, but that it loses out to its rivals as each new product ages, the market for it grows, and the required knowledge is diffused among other countries. The United States may have to race ahead in technology merely to stand still in world markets.

One part of a nation's capital stock is embodied in its labor force as agricultural, industrial, or scientific skill. Another part is embodied in physical equipment: roads, airports, harbors and dams; trucks, aircraft, ships and turbines; farm, factory and office buildings; tractors, lathes, conveyers and typewriters. These are part of the nation's past output that was reserved for investment rather than consumption.

Notice, in passing, that natural and man-made resources can interact powerfully. Bauxite was not a valued natural resource until the development of the electrolytic process for extracting aluminum and of cheap electric power to fuel that process. And aluminum itself was not very valuable until the metalworking industries found ways to use it. Pitchblende was a geological curiosity until man's skill and malevolence found a use for uranium and a way to separate one isotope from others. Population also interacts with technology. Modern mass-production methods need mass markets and are apt to take root first in regions of dense settlement which provide an outlet for large lots of standardized products. Those regions are then apt to enjoy a comparative advantage in the export of these products. Their costs may be lower than those of regions that start later or on a smaller scale. In fact, comparative advantage always has a time dimension. It depends on the state of technology at a given moment and on its subsequent diffusion. It also depends on the history of capital accumulation and, therefore, on the rate of economic growth.

To show how a difference in technique or resources can call forth foreign trade, consider two countries, America and Britain, which are identical in all ways but one: Both of them have 120 man-days of labor available. Both use 2 man-days of labor to grow a ton of potatoes and have enough arable land to use all their workers in potato-farming. But America's coal deposits are just 20 feet down and only 1 man-day of labor is required to dig out a ton, while Britain's are 100 feet down and 4 man-days of labor are required to dig out a ton.

If the entire American labor force were employed growing potatoes, it could produce 60 tons per day; 2 man-days of labor are needed to grow a single ton and 120 man-days of labor are available. If, instead, the labor force were employed digging coal, America could produce 120 tons per day; 1 man-day is needed to dig out a single ton and 120 man-days are available. If, finally, America wished to produce both potatoes and coal, it could secure any one of several combinations. To produce a single ton of coal, it would have to divert 1 man-day of labor from its potato fields and, therefore, reduce potato output by half a ton. To produce 2 tons of coal, it would have to divert 2 man-days from the potato fields and reduce potato output by 1 ton.

American *production possibilities* are summarized by line AB in Fig. 2. The distance OA measures coal output when the entire labor force is working in the coal mines (120 tons); the distance OB measures potato output when the entire labor force is working in the potato fields. Points along the line AB describe the combinations of coal and potatoes that can be produced simultaneously. At point P, for example, America produces Oc coal and Od potatoes. It obtains Oc coal by foregoing Bd potatoes.

The slope (steepness) of the line AB measures a vital price relationship—the price of coal expressed in terms of potatoes. Since labor is the only

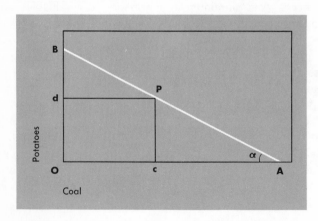

FIG. 2 American production possibilities. The line AB shows how many tons of potatoes America can grow for a chosen level of coal production. If America produces Oc tons of coal, it can grow Od tons of potatoes. The steepness of AB (measured by angle α) gives the price of coal in terms of potatoes.

variable input (factor of production) in this simple model, prices will depend on labor requirements. But 1 man-day of labor is required to mine a ton of coal and 2 man-days are needed to grow a ton of potatoes. Hence, a ton of coal is half as costly as a ton of potatoes. The diagram records this fact; OB is half as long as OA.[1]

If, then, America could not trade with the outside world, it would have to consume some combination of coal and potatoes lying on AB in Fig. 2, and a ton of coal would be worth half a ton of potatoes.

Britain also needs 2 man-days of labor to produce a ton of potatoes and could consequently grow 60 tons if it used all its labor in its potato patches. But it needs 4 man-days of labor to dig out a ton of coal and could only mine 30 tons if it used all its labor in its coal mines. Finally, Britain could produce a single ton of coal by diverting 4 man-days of labor from potato-growing, thereby giving up 2 tons of potatoes.

[1] One can arrive at this same result by examining marginal costs. If product markets are perfectly competitive, prices must equal marginal costs. If labor is the only variable input and labor requirements are constant for all output levels, marginal costs must equal labor requirements per unit of extra output multiplied by the wage rate. Hence:

Price of Coal = Marginal Cost of Coal = Wage Rate × Man-days of Labor Needed to Produce a Ton of Coal

Price of Potatoes = Marginal Cost of Potatoes = Wage Rate × Man-days of Labor Needed to Produce a Ton of Potatoes

Therefore:

$$\frac{\text{Price of Coal}}{\text{Price of Potatoes}} = \frac{\text{Man-days Needed to Produce a Ton of Coal}}{\text{Man-days Needed to Produce a Ton of Potatoes}}$$

The wage rate cancels out in this calculation, as it must be the same in both industries.

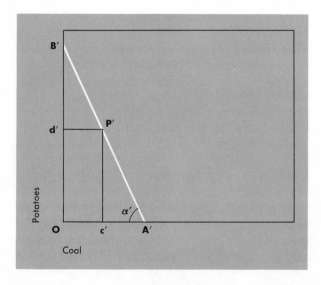

FIG. 3 British production possibilities. The line A'B' shows how many tons of potatoes Britain can grow for a chosen level of coal production. The steepness of A'B' (measured by angle a') gives the price of coal in terms of potatoes. Britain can produce as many potatoes as America, but far less coal. The price of coal in Britain is much higher than in America.

Britain's production possibilities are described by the line A'B' in Fig. 3. Maximum potato output, OB', is the same as in America, because the two countries have the same amounts of labor and are equally efficient at potato-growing. But maximum coal output, OA', is smaller in Britain than in America, for Britain's coal lies much deeper in the ground.

The line A'B' is much steeper than AB in Fig. 2. This difference is explained by the difference in mining costs. British coal must be twice as expensive as British potatoes, for labor costs are twice as high. Hence, OB' is twice as long as OA'.

Isolated from the outside world, Britain would produce some combination of coal and potatoes lying on A'B', and a ton of coal would be worth 2 tons of potatoes.

But now suppose that America and Britain are allowed to trade and that goods can move between them without any cost. The opportunity for trade will create a single Anglo-American market and, therefore, a single price for coal. This new common price will lie between the national extremes —less than the prior British price (two tons of potatoes for a ton of coal) and higher than the prior American price (half a ton of potatoes for a ton of coal).[2] Britain can now obtain a ton of coal without giving up as many potatoes as it had to sacrifice to produce its own coal. It will tend to specialize in potato-growing and use its potatoes to buy American coal. America is

[2] The new common price for coal could also settle at one national extreme. In this case, one country would capture all the gains from trade, but the other would be no worse off than without any trade. If the price came to rest at the old British level, America would garner all the gains from trade; it would get its potatoes cheaper than it could at home. If the price came to rest at the old American level, Britain would garner all the gains from trade; it would get its coal cheaper than it could at home.

FIG. 4   Trade between America and Britain. Before trade, America produced Oc coal and Od potatoes, consuming all it produced. Britain produced O'c' coal and O'd' potatoes, consuming all it produced. When trade is opened, America produces OA coal and no potatoes; Britain produces O'B' potatoes and no coal. America consumes Oe coal and exports eA coal to buy British potatoes; Britain consumes O'f' potatoes and exports f'B' potatoes to buy American coal. America can then consume Of potatoes (Of being equal to f'B' British exports); Britain can consume O'e' coal (O'e' being equal to eA American exports). Each country can consume more of both products than it did before trade. The price of coal, shown by the angle Θ, is higher than the pre-trade American price (the slope of AB), but lower than the pre-trade British price (the slope of A'B').

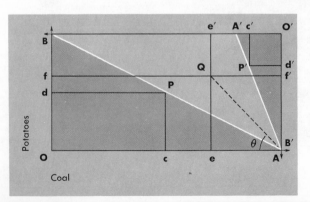

able to obtain more potatoes for its coal. It will tend to specialize in coal-mining and use its coal to buy British potatoes.

To illustrate this rearrangement of production, suppose that the common coal price is stabilized at 1 ton of potatoes for a ton of coal. Britain can import a ton of coal by growing and exporting 1 ton of potatoes. Without trade, by contrast, it had to sacrifice 2 tons of potatoes to produce a ton of coal. In effect, Britain saves 2 man-days of labor on each ton of coal consumed. For its part, America can import a ton of potatoes by mining and exporting 1 ton of coal. Without trade, it had to sacrifice 2 tons of coal to produce a ton of potatoes. America saves 1 man-day of labor on each ton of potatoes consumed.

Figure 4 restates these results with greater generality. There, the left-hand triangle is the American production-possibilities line, just as it appeared in Fig. 2. The righthand triangle is Britain's production-possibilities line, taken from Fig. 3 but flipped upside down. If America and Britain cannot trade, each is confined to its own production-possibilities line, America at P and Britain at P'. If they are allowed to trade, they can rearrange production and consumption to mutual advantage. America can specialize in coal-mining, using all its labor to produce OA tons. Britain can specialize in potato-farming, using all its labor to produce O'B' tons. America can then consume Oe tons of coal and export eA tons to pay for potatoes. Britain can consume O'f' tons of potatoes and export f'B' tons to pay for coal. America can buy Of tons of potatoes (equal to the f'B' Britain will export), and Britain can buy O'e' tons of coal (equal to the eA tons America will export). American consumption has moved from P to Q, and British consumption has moved from P' to Q. Each country can consume more of both goods than it did before trade.[3]

Figure 4 shows two ways to view the gains from trade. First, it shows that every country can escape the confines of its own resource endowment. Before trade, each country consumed a combination of coal and potatoes lying on its own production-possibilities line. Its choices were restricted by its resource endowment. But trade allows every country to reshuffle output and consume a combination of commodities it could never produce by itself. The individual consumer has a wider range of choice. Figure 4 also shows that trade enlarges global output by allowing every country to specialize. Before trade, coal output was Oc *plus* c'O'. With trade it rises to OA (an increase of ce *plus* e'c'). Before trade, potato output was Od plus d'O'. With trade, it rises

---

[3] The situation described in Fig. 4 is not the only possibility. The point Q could settle down anywhere within the unshaded part of the diagram, depending on demand conditions. Furthermore, Q could come to rest on AB or A'B'. These are the extreme cases mentioned in the last footnote. If Q came to rest on AB, Britain would specialize completely and take all the gains from trade. America would tend to specialize in coal, but would also grow potatoes. If Q came to rest on A'B', America would specialize completely and take all the gains from trade. Britain would tend to specialize in potatoes, but would also mine coal.

to O'B' (an increase of df *plus* f'd'). This increase in output was required for each country to increase its consumption of both commodities. It also leads to a basic proposition in international economics: *Free trade is the best regime for the world as a whole.* The increase in coal and potato output shown by Fig. 4 is the largest increase possible. Hence free trade allocates economic tasks to maximize world output and income.

PRODUCTIVITY, WAGES, AND PRICES

Figure 4 shows the new common price of coal as the slope (steepness) of the dotted line AQ. This line is steeper than AB, but flatter than A'B'. Coal has become more expensive in America, but cheaper than it was in Britain. But you have not seen how this common price comes into being. To study this important process, you must look at wages, prices, and exchange rates.

Suppose, then, that the American wage rate stands at $15 per man-day, while the British wage rate stands at £5. A ton of American potatoes will cost $30 (2 man-days of labor are needed to grow a ton), and a ton of coal will cost $15 (1 man-day of labor is needed to mine a ton). A ton of British potatoes will cost £10 (2 man-days of labor are needed to grow a ton), and a ton of coal will cost £20 (4 man-days of labor are needed to mine a ton).

Now suppose that trade is opened and that the exchange rate between the dollar and the pound is set by international agreement at $3 per pound. The dollar price of British potatoes will be $30 per ton; the dollar price of British coal will be $60 per ton. Neither country will have reason to import potatoes, for the dollar prices are the same. But Britain will begin to import coal from America, since British coal costs $60 a ton while American coal costs $15 a ton.

If both countries' workers were fully employed before trade began, there will be an excess demand for labor in America because of the British demand for American coal. There will also be unemployment in Britain because of the shift in British demand from domestic to foreign coal. Wage rates will rise in America and fall in Britain. This change in wages, however, will make British potatoes cheaper than American, and both countries' consumers will start to buy their potatoes in Britain. British farmers will plant larger crops, taking up the labor released from the British coal mines; American farmers will cut back their crops, releasing labor to the American mines.

This process will only cease when unemployment disappears in the British coal mines and the labor shortage ends in the American coal mines. These things will happen when consumers have rearranged their purchases, responding to the price changes that result from the wage changes. And when the wage changes have ceased, the price of American coal will be higher than it was to start (because of the increase in American wages), while the price of British potatoes will be lower than it was to start (because of the decrease in British wages). The wage-rate changes will have offset America's higher productivity, allowing Britain's comparative advantage in potato-growing to show through in a lower price.

The reallocation of resources induced by trade will also take place when many countries and many products are involved. Look at the three center columns in Fig. 5. They describe cost structures in three countries, I, II, and III, each one making 4 products before trade begins. The letters w_1, w_2, and w_3 stand for the national wage rates (expressed in a common currency by using exchange rates). I have aligned them to assume that wage rates are the same before trade begins. The vertical distances to a, b, c, etc., represent production costs for the 4 commodities so that a is the cheapest item in country I, b is next, and c is more expensive still. The distances between

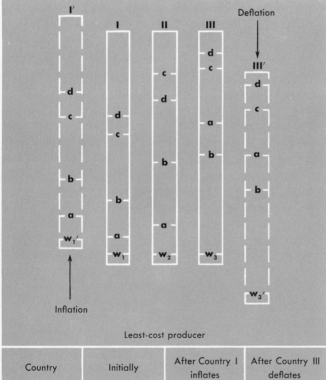

FIG. 5 A three-country, four-product model. Before the wage-rate adjustments in countries I and II, country I has the lowest money costs in all 4 commodities. After country I inflates (raising its wage rate and shifting its column upwards like I′), country II gains a cost advantage in products a and d. After country III deflates (lowering its wage rate and shifting its column downward, like III′), it secures a cost advantage in product b.

Least-cost producer

Country	Initially	After Country I inflates	After Country III deflates
I	a, b, c, d	b, c	c
II		a, d	a, d
III			b

the letters refer to the cost ratios, not to cost differences in dollars and cents. This means that an increase in a country's wage rate will thrust up its whole column, but will not alter the positions of the letters in the column.

Notice, now, that country I would have the lowest money costs for all 4 products if the 3 countries' wage rates were the same; a in I is lower than a in II and lower still than a in III. Likewise for b, c, and d. But this situation could not last after trade had begun. The pressures of domestic and foreign demand would raise w_1 and the corresponding short fall in demand would depress w_2 and w_3. This process is symbolized by the position of column I'. It is identical to column I but thrust upward to denote a higher wage rate. Now country II is the low-cost source for products a and d, but country I still has an advantage in b and c, and country III has nothing to sell. There must and will be more inflation in countries I and II, or more deflation in country III. This further change is symbolized by the position of column III'. It is the same as column III but thrust downward to denote a lower wage rate. Country III has now found an advantage in the production of item b, even though it is the least efficient producer of every item on the list. The wage-rate adjustments—upward in country I and downward in country III—have "washed out" the over-all differences in national efficiency, leaving differences in relative internal costs to create a beneficial trade pattern.

SOME EVIDENCE

Statistical studies of trade and productivity show that the *Principle of Comparative Advantage* can explain actual trade patterns. Output per worker is much lower in Great Britain than in the United States, but average British wages are also much lower. The over-all difference in wage rates offsets the over-all difference in efficiency. Trade flows are consequently governed by wide variations in comparative efficiency from one domestic industry to the next.

A British economist, Sir Donald MacDougall, studied transatlantic trade before the Second World War, looking at 24 separate industries. His results are summarized at the top of Table 1. In every case, American output per worker was higher than British output per worker. But it was 5.4 times as high in the production of electric light bulbs and only 1.1 times as high in the production of cement. By contrast, average American wage rates were twice as high as average British wage rates. Whenever, then, British workers were more than half as efficient as their American rivals, British goods could compete in the United States; British exports to the United States were larger than American exports to Britain. When, instead, British productivity was less than half as high as American, the corresponding U.S. industry had the cost advantage, and in 7 out of 12 such cases, American exports to Britain were larger than British exports to the United States.

These results show up again in the post-war period. An American economist, Robert Stern, has reworked MacDougall's example using trade and labor data for 1950. At that time, U.S. wage rates were about three times as high as British wage rates. When, however, U.S. labor productivity was more than three times British productivity, American exports were usually larger than British exports. Stern has also studied a larger sample comprising 39 manufacturing industries. In 15 of these 39 cases, U.S. labor was more than three times as efficient as British labor, and in 11 of these 15 cases, U.S. exports to Britain were larger than British exports to the United States. In the other 24 cases, U.S. productivity was higher than British, but not as much as three times as high. In 21 of these 24 cases, British exports to the United States were larger than American exports to Britain. Stern's results are also summarized in Table 1. The middle section (B) gives 1950 data for the same 24 industries studied by MacDougall; the final section (C) gives 1950 data for Stern's larger sample.

TABLE 1

Output per Worker and Transatlantic Exports, Great Britain and the United States

		Number of Industries	
Difference in Labor Productivity	Total	In Which U.S. Exports Larger than British	In Which U.S. Exports Smaller than British
A. Pre-war trade (13 industries): U.S. wages double British wages			
U.S. output per worker more than double British	12	7	5
U.S. output per worker not more than double British	12	0	12
B. Post-war trade (24 industries): U.S. wages treble British wages			
U.S. output per worker more than treble British	7	5	2
U.S. output per worker not more than treble British	17	2	15
C. Post-war-trade (39 industries): U.S. wages treble British wages			
U.S. output per worker more than treble British	15	11	4
U.S output per worker not more than treble British	24	3	21

Source: Robert M. Stern, "British and American Productivity and Comparative Costs in International Trade," *Oxford Economic Papers,* Vol. 14, No. 3 (October, 1962), pp. 278, 288.

These uniformities are striking indeed. The number of exceptions is very small, especially in Stern's large sample. One would, in fact, expect many more exceptions. Remember that most countries impose barriers to foreign trade that interfere with the Principle of Comparative Advantage. Furthermore, each of the product classes studied includes several distinct items, and one must allow for differences in quality. Finally, labor costs are not the only major costs, so that labor productivity is not the only cause of trade. If high U.S. output per worker were entirely due to the use of machinery, the U.S. advantage in efficiency would be partly offset by higher payments for the use and maintenance of that machinery.

MORE COMPLEX MODELS

The two-country, two-product, labor-cost model I employed at the start of this chapter is much like the one used by David Ricardo early in the nineteenth century. The multi-country, multi-commodity version was first employed by F. Y. Edgeworth at the end of the century. Both models help to explain the gains from trade and the price and cost adjustments which must be made so that trade can be sustained. But they shed much less light on other major problems—the role of international differences in factor supplies, the impact of economic growth on the structure of foreign trade, and the impact of trade on the income distribution. These problems can be examined only by using models that employ several factors of production—land, labor, and machines.

The multi-factor model I shall use derives from work by two Swedish economists, Eli Heckscher and Bertil Ohlin. Like the models you have already met, it excludes economics of scale, neglects transport costs, and assumes that tastes are the same in every country. But it allows for several inputs (factors of production) and thereby shows how trade may arise from international differences in factor supplies.

The *factor-endowments approach* to trade theory begins by assuming that products have different factor requirements. Cars demand more machine time (capital) per worker than, say, cotton cloth or furniture, and missiles more machine time than cars or cotton cloth. The technique used to make cars can be described by a steep line like the one labeled "cars" in Fig. 6. The

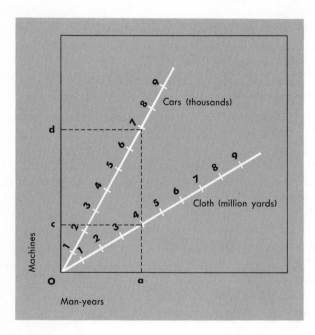

FIG. 6 Labor and capital requirements: cotton cloth and cars. The two lines show amount of output from using labor and machines. Cars are more capital-intensive than cloth because they use more machine time per man-year of labor.

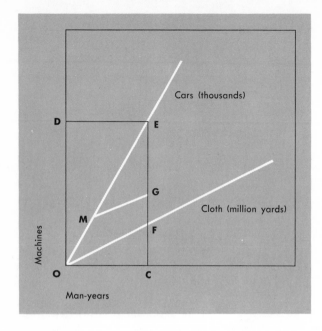

FIG. 7 The interaction of technology and factor endowments. A country with OC man-years of labor and OD machines could produce OE cars or OF million yards of cloth. It could also produce OM cars and MG million yards of cloth. It is well-endowed for making cars (the capital-intensive product) and poorly endowed for making cloth (the labor-intensive product).

technique used to make cloth can be described by a flat line like the one labeled "cloth" in the same diagram. A cloth manufacturer making 4 million yards a year will need Oa man-years of labor and the services of Oc machines. An automobile manufacturer making 7,000 cars would also need Oa man-years, but will use Od machines. His is the more *capital-intensive* method of production.[4]

The models then assume that all countries have full access to the same technology, but differ in their factor endowments. One country may have more labor than another, but far fewer machines or less farm land. Countries will consequently differ in their ability to produce the several goods they consume and will benefit from trade.

Consider another simple example—a country having very little labor but well-endowed with machines. Its supplies of these two factors can be described by a box like OCED in Fig. 7. It has OC man-years of labor and OD machines (each machine being able to supply services that can be used in any industry). This country could use all its resources making cars and turn out OE thousand cars a year. This procedure would employ every ma-

[4] One could, of course, make cars by several methods, more or less capital-intensive. One could use a small machine shop or an automated plant. One also could weave cloth by many methods, some of them quite highly mechanized. The choice of technique will depend on the prices of the inputs—the wage rates paid to workers and the rental price of machinery (the interest costs of capital and an allowance for repair and depreciation). But the factor-endowments models assume that the product which is the more capital-intensive at one set of factor prices is also the more capital-intensive at every other set. If, for example, labor grew more costly tomorrow, the cloth manufacturer might shift to a more intensive use of machinery; the line marked "cloth" in Fig. 6 would get somewhat steeper. But the auto industry would also change its technique, so that the line marked "cars" would also become steeper.

19

chine and the entire labor force.[5] Alternatively, it could devote all its resources to producing cloth, but could only turn out OF million yards, since it does not have the labor to produce any more. Finally, it could make some cars and some cloth. It could produce OM thousand cars, then move along a new "cloth" line (parallel to OF) to weave MG million yards of cloth. Whatever its output mix, however, the country must choose between an extra car or yard of cloth, just as America and Britain had to choose between coal and potatoes in our first example. The country will confront a production-possibilities line whose shape depends on its supplies of labor and machinery and on the available technology.

A country with more labor and fewer machines would face a different production-possibilities line. It could produce more cloth than the country examined in Fig. 7, and could increase its cloth production at a smaller sacrifice of automobiles. Its price of cloth would be lower when expressed in terms of cars.

If, then, two countries have different endowments of labor and machinery, both of them can gain from trade. The country with abundant labor and few machines can specialize in cloth production and export its speciality in order to import cars. The country with little labor and abundant machinery can specialize in cars and export its speciality in order to import cloth. Trade allows each country to obtain those goods it is ill-equipped to make—those which make the heaviest demands on its scarce factors of production. Free trade, moreover, will be best from the standpoint of the world as a whole. It will work to maximize global output by fostering efficient specialization. The country with a relative abundance of labor can increase its cloth output at small cost in terms of cars. Taken together, these adjustments can enlarge world output, giving consumers more cars and more cloth.

TRADE AND FACTOR PRICES

The model I have used to introduce modern theory has one peculiar feature. Changes in the composition of each country's output cause variations in its total employment. If the country represented by Fig. 7 produces any cloth at all, it will have idle machinery. If it produces OF million yards, it will have EF idle machines; if it produces MG million yards, it will have EG idle machines. These variations in factor use result from the very strict limits I imposed on technology. Figure 7 shows just one way to make cars and one way to make cloth. If a country could choose from several methods for producing cars and from several more for producing cloth, changes in the output mix would change factor prices (wages and the rental charges for machinery) rather than employment.

[5] This is a very special result. It is built into the diagram by drawing OCED to touch the "cars" line just at E. In the more general case, the point E could lie above or below the "cars" line. But this would make the argument more complicated without altering the principal conclusions.

If the country represented by Fig. 7 started out making cars and cloth and used the methods shown in the diagram, some of its machinery would stand idle. But if this situation continued for long, the owners of machines would bid down rental rates to secure employment for their machines. And if manufacturers were free to alter their techniques, they would respond to lower rental charges by adopting more capital-intensive methods of production in every industry. They would replace labor with machinery.

When this sort of *factor substitution* is possible, the model changes in two ways. First, the production-possibilities curve bends outward like XQPY in Fig. 8, instead of being a straight line like the ones in Figs. 2 and 3. Second, the price of cars expressed in terms of cloth depends on the output mix, being equal to the slope of XQPY at the point of actual production. If, for example, production were at P, involving Ox_1 thousand cars and Oy_1 million yards of cloth, the price of cars in terms of cloth would equal the slope of XQPY at P. If, instead, production were at Q, involving Ox_2 thousand cars and Oy_2 million yards of cloth, the price of cars would then equal the slope of XQPY at Q.

Notice, now, that XQPY is steeper at Q than at P, implying a higher price for cars. Notice, too, that more cars are made at Q than at P. The price of cars must go up to increase production. This link between prices and pro-

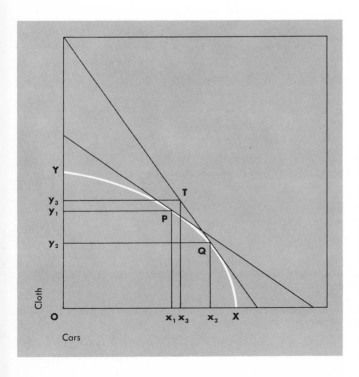

Cloth

Cars

FIG. 8 The production-possibilities curve with variable techniques. With a transformation curve like XQPY, a country can produce and consume at P (making Ox_1 cars and Oy_1 cloth); the price of cars in terms of cloth will then be equal to the slope of XQPY at P. With trade at a higher price for cars, production will shift to Q (Ox_2 cars and Oy_2 cloth), and consumption will shift to T (Ox_3 cars and Oy_3 cloth). The country will export x_2x_3 cars and import y_2y_3 cloth.

duction arises from the difference in capital-intensities as between the two industries. Since cars are more capital-intensive than cloth, a switch from cloth to car production augments the demand for machines. The automobile industry will always use more machines per worker than the cloth industry is able to release. An increase in the demand for machines, however, will bid up the rental charge for machinery, and an increase in the rental charge will raise the price of cars more than it raises the price of cloth, because cars use more machinery than cloth.

There is, in fact, a strong connection between prevailing product prices (cars and cloth) and prevailing factor prices (labor and machines), and this connection has an intriguing implication: *Free trade will tend to equalize factor prices across all trading countries.* Suppose there are two countries, Fewmen and Manymen. Fewmen has little labor but much machinery; Manymen is well-endowed with labor but has little machinery. If the two countries have similar tastes and each is compelled to satisfy its own needs, wages will be high in Fewmen relative to rental charges on machines, while wages will be low in Manymen relative to rental charges. If the two countries can trade, Fewmen can relieve its shortage of labor and its wages will fall relative to rental charges. Manymen can relieve its shortage of machines and its wages will rise relative to rental charges. This, in fact, is what free trade will do: As wages would be relatively high in Fewmen before trade, cloth would be expensive compared to cars. With the opening of trade, Fewmen will therefore export cars and import cloth. It will increase its car production and cut back its cloth production. These shifts in production will augment Fewmen's demand for machines and reduce its demand for labor. Manymen will increase its cloth production and cut back its car production. These shifts will augment its demand for labor and reduce its demand for machines. If there are no transport costs, free trade will equalize product prices in Fewmen and Manymen. It will also equalize the two countries' factor prices.

In actual fact, of course, factor prices are not equal around the world—and the differences are too large to be explained by transport costs and trade barriers. Hence, the simple model I have used cannot be perfectly applicable to the real world. It may ignore important economies of scale and the fact that modern technology is not available to every country. But the *tendency* described by the model—the role of trade in *reducing* factor-price differences—may still be quite important.[6]

[6] Furthermore, the statistics may exaggerate international differences in factor prices. When we compare wage rates around the world, we are comparing rather different things. Some countries' wage statistics are heavily weighted with the large returns to skill; others' may refer to the lower wages of unskilled labor. If one were to compare the wage rates of equally skilled workers, of equally fine land, and so on, being sure to match like with like, factor prices might prove more nearly equal than they usually appear.

TRADE AND FACTOR MOVEMENTS

Suppose, again, that goods could not move between the two countries. Wages would be higher in Fewmen than in Manymen. If, then, workers could travel without cost, there would be migration from Manymen to Fewmen; and if this migration were to continue for as long as wage rates differed, it would make the two countries very much alike. Fewmen would wind up with more machines *and* more labor, but the *ratio* of man-years to machine-years would be equal in the two countries. This is because the wage-rate difference would persist as long as the ratio of men to machines were lower in Fewmen than in Manymen. It would not vanish until the ratios became equal. Hence, the migration caused by the wage difference would have to continue until Manymen and Fewmen had similar endowments.

This analysis suggests another way to look at the gains from trade. It argues that free trade can sometimes substitute for international movements of labor and capital. Factor movements and free trade both reduce differences in factor prices. Factor movements do so by erasing differences in the national endowments. Free trade does so by offsetting those differences. Trade eliminates the need for a redistribution of the factors by reallocating economic tasks. It allows every country to make the best use of its own peculiar factor endowment.

The Use and Abuse of Tariffs

All the models you have seen illustrate the same basic proposition: Free trade maximizes world output. Furthermore, the models show that free trade benefits each participating nation. Every country can escape the confines of its own resource endowment to consume a collection of commodities better than the best it can produce.

Why, then, do we still hear so much clamor for protective tariffs and other trade barriers? The answer to this question has two parts: Many fallacious arguments against foreign trade are easily refuted but keep bobbing up. Economists can demolish the protectionists' arguments, but speeches about "cheap foreign labor" and the "national defense" have great popular appeal. Then there are several arguments for tariffs that survive rigorous analysis. Free trade may be best for the world as a whole, but it may not be best from a single country's standpoint. Tariffs and other trade barriers may sometimes be employed to redistribute gains from trade in favor of one country, to redistribute income within a single country, to raise domestic employment, or to facilitate economic development.

THE HARDY FALLACIES

Every so often someone will tell you that the United States must use tariffs to protect itself from cheap foreign labor. He is armed with lots of figures about low foreign wages, and his numbers are usually accurate. But his inference is totally wrong. In fact, you encountered the answer to his argument when you learned how trading prices are determined. The very first example in this chapter assumed that British and American wages were equal before the start of trade. British wages were £5 a day and the exchange rate stood at $3 per pound, so that British and American wages worked out at $15 a day. But when trade was opened, excess demand raised American wages, and unemployment reduced British wages. This result was not a caprice of the market. It served a necessary function. If British wages had not fallen, British potato prices would not have declined, and Britain could not have sold potatoes to import coal. The change in wage rates offset Britain's lower productivity and was vital to the adjustment process that attends the opening of trade.

The "cheap foreign labor" argument for tariffs neglects this important link between wages and efficiency. It regards a systematic wage-rate difference as an unfair competitive handicap when, in truth, the difference is required for trade to take place. The wage-rate difference translates comparative advantage into price, and prices guide the flow of trade.

Other protectionists argue for tariffs to defend the national security—to preserve those domestic industries that will produce guns and planes when war breaks out. This may be the oldest argument in the protectionists' arsenal, and made sense some time ago. A country that did not have a steel industry could not make tanks or cannon if cut off from imports. But the argument makes no sense in the thermonuclear age. A nation's ability to protect itself against aggression no longer depends on its industrial capacity. It would not have time to mobilize its industry as in the Second World War, so that peacetime productive capacity is virtually irrelevant to national security.[7]

TARIFFS AND THE DISTRIBUTION OF THE GAINS FROM TRADE

But what of the "respectable" arguments for tariffs—those that appeal to national gain and survive analysis? One such argument asserts that a country can extract larger gains from trade by imposing tariffs on goods from abroad. This particular argument is quite sound and much like the proposition that a monopolist can increase his profits by restricting his sales. By limiting its imports with a tax, a country can sometimes force down the price

---

[7] One must, of course, contemplate the possibility of "limited" war like the Korean War. But such a war is not likely to cut this country off from vital raw materials or finished manufactures. If, indeed, it were that widespread, it could hardly be contained or fought with conventional weapons. A war that was sufficiently general to isolate this country from its key suppliers would "escalate" very rapidly indeed.

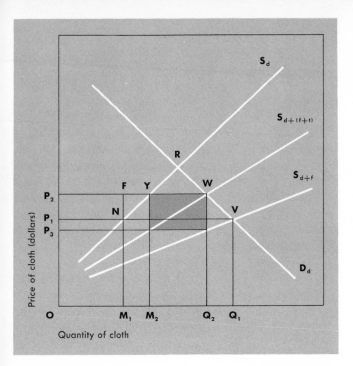

Price of cloth (dollars)

Quantity of cloth

S_d

$S_{d+(f+t)}$

R

F Y W

S_{d+f}

P_2

N

V

P_1
P_3

D_d

O M₁ M₂ Q₂ Q₁

FIG. 9 The impact of a tariff on Fewmen's imports and production. A tariff shifts the home-and-import supply curve from S_{d+f} to $S_{d+(f+t)}$, raising the domestic price of cloth from OP_1 to OP_2, but lowering the import price from OP_1 to OP_3. Import volume falls from M_1Q_1 to M_2Q_2 because of the drop in consumption (Q_1Q_2) and the substitution of domestic for foreign cloth (M_1M_2).

at which other countries sell to it. It can improve its *terms of trade.* If, of course, it carries the process too far, the loss it suffers by restricting its consumption of imported products will exceed the gain it takes by reducing foreign prices. The monopolist faces an analogous danger; if he cuts back output too much, he loses more on volume than he gains on price. But a country that enjoys a strategic position in world trade can rearrange the gains from trade in its own favor by judicious use of import restrictions.

Figure 9 illustrates this process, showing trade in cotton cloth between Fewmen and Manymen. As in an ordinary supply-and-demand diagram, the price of cloth is listed on the vertical axis and the quantity is listed on the horizontal axis. The line D_d is Fewmen's demand curve for cloth. The line S_d is Fewmen's supply curve of cloth. The point R locates the situation that would prevail without foreign trade, as Fewmen would then have to rely on its own supply of cloth.

Look, next, at the line S_{d+f}. It shows the supply of cloth available to Fewmen from domestic *and* foreign sources combined—from Fewmen's producers and Manymen's exporters. The combined supply curve is the one that would prevail with free trade, and V locates the free-trade equilibrium. The price of cloth would be OP_1 dollars, and the total consumption in Fewmen would be OQ_1. Fewmen would produce OM_1 at home (for this is its domestic output at the free-trade price) and would import M_1Q_1 from Manymen.

Now suppose that Fewmen imposes a 30 per cent tariff on imported cloth; its government intercepts 30 per cent of its citizens' expenditure on

25

imported cloth. A 30 per cent import tariff can be described by raising the supply curve S_{d+f} by 30 per cent, until it looks like $S_{d+(t+t)}$. The new equilibrium will be at W, and the domestic price of cloth will rise to OP_2 dollars. This price increase will reduce Fewmen's total cloth consumption, but will stimulate domestic production. Imports will be squeezed by the fall in consumption and by the rise in domestic production, declining to M_2Q_2. At the same time, however, the supply price of foreign cloth (of imports from Manymen) will drop all the way to OP_3. The *terms of trade* will shift in Fewmen's favor.

To complete the analysis, you would have next to allow for the impact of the tax on Fewmen's fiscal policies. Fewmen's government collects P_2P_3 dollars of tax per million yards of imported cloth, or a total tax equal to the area of the shaded rectangle. It can spend this extra revenue or remit it to the public by lowering some other tax. The final equilibrium position will depend on the way the revenue is spent. Even as it stands, however, Fig. 9 offers a powerful presumption that Fewmen can gain by taxing cloth imports. Although its own consumers pay more for cloth than they did with free trade, they pay less to the foreign producers.

In general, a country can capture a larger share of the gains from trade if the foreign supply curve slopes upward and if the foreigner does not retaliate by imposing tariffs of his own. If the foreign supply curve were horizontal, the supply price of imports would not fall (the *terms of trade* would not improve). If the foreigner were to retaliate, he might recoup all his losses, but then might provoke Fewmen to impose another round of tariffs. In the end, both countries could lose out, for the global gains from trade shrink as trade is reduced by each successive round of tariffs. Yet governments have been tempted to use tariffs to improve the *terms of trade,* and a free-trade situation may not endure unless it is reinforced by treaties that bar the use of tariffs.

TARIFFS AND THE DISTRIBUTION OF DOMESTIC INCOME

Tariffs can also be used to alter the domestic distribution of income. Remember that the product-price differences that give rise to trade have their clear counterparts in factor-price differences. Remember, too, that free trade tends to equalize product prices between the participating countries and, therefore, to equalize factor prices.

Now turn the argument on end. Starting with free trade and equal factor prices as between Fewmen and Manymen, let Fewmen impose its 30 per cent tariff on imported cloth. This, you have seen, will raise the price of cloth in Fewmen and lower it in Manymen. It will therefore raise the wage rate in Fewmen and lower the rental rate on machinery. The tariff will encourage Fewmen's cloth production and will discourage car production, for Fewmen's auto exports will contract with the drop in its cloth imports. The tariff will consequently increase Fewmen's demand for labor (the input used intensively in cloth production) and will lower its demand for machinery (the input used intensively in car production). It will raise Fewmen's wage rates and reduce Fewmen's rental rates on machinery. It will redistribute income in favor of labor.[8]

EQUITY AND EFFICIENCY

Thus far, you have seen how tariffs redistribute income between countries and within them. Trade restrictions, however, are a haphazard way to achieve redistribution. Countries with the market power to affect the *terms of trade* by imposing tariffs—and the internal pressure groups that influence legislative processes—do not necessarily deserve aid through redistribution. Furthermore, tariffs are an inefficient way to redistribute income because they eat away a part of the pie they are redividing. They sacrifice production to secure equity.

This conclusion follows directly from what you know about free trade. If free trade maximizes global output, any deviation from free trade will reduce production, leaving less to go around. Figure 9 illustrates this point. It shows that a tariff replaces low-cost imports with high-cost domestic production. The last unit of domestic cloth costs OP_2 dollars to produce (for price equals marginal cost). The last unit of imported cloth costs OP_3 dollars to produce. Domestic cloth is more costly to the world as a whole.

TARIFFS AND EMPLOYMENT

I have tried to show how tariffs can be used to affect the allocation of resources and the distribution of income. They may also be imposed to affect the *utilization* of resources—the levels of employment and production.

When two countries start to trade, they may not strike an equilibrium right away. One country's prices may be higher than the other's when they are compared at the going exchange rate, and that country will have to reduce its wage rates. If it cannot cut costs by cutting wages, its least efficient industries will shrink, but its more efficient industries will not grow to take up the slack. It will trade from a point *inside* its production-possibilities curve, not from a point *on* the curve, and free trade may be worse than no trade at all.

If, then, wage rates and other costs are very rigid, a country may gain by restricting its foreign trade. Tariffs will divert demand from foreign to domestic goods, raising output and employment. This result is most likely if the

---

[8] This argument has its (approximate) counterpart in Fig. 9. The increase in domestic cloth production (OM_1 to OM_2) caused by the tariff raises the incomes of the factors of production already employed in the cloth industry, even as it adds to production and employment in that industry. Under free trade, the industry was earning a gross income equal to OP_1NM_1. With a tariff, it will earn OP_2YM_2. The increase can be broken down into two parts: M_1FYM_2, which goes to the newly employed factors of production (those that produce the extra cloth M_1M_2), and P_1P_2FN, which goes to the factors of production *already* employed in making cloth (those that produced the original OM_1 of cloth).

country's unemployed resources are concentrated in its import-competing industries. Tariffs can even combat unemployment when it is not caused by wage and price discrepancies but, instead, by a decline in domestic demand during the business cycle.

Once again, however, tariffs are inefficient instruments. They can only raise employment by expanding the import-competing industries, not the more efficient export industries. Far better, then, to foster wage-rate flexibility or, what may be simpler, to change the exchange rate until the high-cost country's prices are aligned with those of its competitors. It should *devalue* its currency by charging its citizens more for a unit of foreign currency and by selling its own currency more cheaply to foreigners. A devaluation increases the domestic price of foreign goods (imports), since foreign currency becomes more expensive. To this extent, it is much like a tariff. But a devaluation also lowers the foreign price of domestic goods (exports), since domestic currency becomes cheaper for foreigners. Unlike a tariff, then, a devaluation stimulates the export industries along with the import-competing industries, and does not distort resource allocation.

To put the same point more strongly—tariffs shift unemployment onto the foreigner, and solve a country's employment problems at the expense of world efficiency. One country's import-competing industries (those that benefit by tariff protection) are another country's export industries (those that make the best use of that country's resource endowment). Tariffs are a "beggar-my-neighbor" remedy for unemployment.

TARIFFS AND ECONOMIC TRANSFORMATION

Most of the standard arguments for tariff protection imply a permanent departure from free trade. One group of arguments, however, advocates a

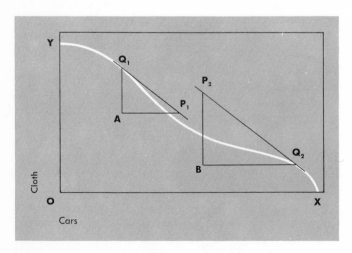

FIG. 10 Increasing returns and the production-possibilities curve. This country could produce at Q_1, export cloth and import cars, and consume at P_1. It would be better off, however, to produce at Q_2, export cars and import cloth, and consume at P_2. To get from Q_1 to Q_2, it may have to impose a temporary tariff on imported cars to encourage the expansion of its own car industry.

temporary deviation. From time to time, it is said, countries must make major changes in production; they must reallocate resources in a large way, not just at the margin. They may find it easier to make the change behind the protection of a tariff wall.

There are two distinct arguments for a *transitional* tariff. One of them promises economies of scale. The other promises economies of age. If costs fall as output grows—if production is subject to economies of scale—the production-possibilities curve may look like XQ_2Q_1Y in Fig. 10, bending *inward* rather than *outward* over part of its total length. Suppose, now, that a country starts out at Q_1, exporting Q_1A million yards of cloth and importing AP_1 thousand cars. It will be better off than without trade, but will not be as well off as it could be at Q_2. There, it could export Q_2B thousand cars, import BP_2 million yards of cloth, and reach P_2, superior to P_1. To move from Q_1 to Q_2, however, the country must expand its auto industry and this may be very difficult. In order to cross the "gully" in its production-possibilities curve, the country must temporarily subsidize or protect its automobile-makers.

The second argument for a transitional tariff urges protection for an "infant industry," and was given its first famous formulation by Alexander Hamilton in his *Report on Manufactures*. A young industry may be less efficient than one which is long established. It may lack seasoned managers, skilled labor, and reliable suppliers of raw materials. Hence, a young industry may warrant protection, but only until it matures and cuts back its unit costs so that it can compete efficiently with foreign producers. In effect, this argument forecasts that temporary aid to young industries will expand the production-possibilities curve after a time, and that world output will then be greater than if there had been no departure from free trade.

Both of these transitional arguments enjoy widespread respect. Neither has any analytical defect. But enormous problems must be solved if they are to be applied correctly. First, one must decide which industries can capture sufficient economies of scale or economies of age to survive after the tariff is removed. If a country protects all its young industries, it will waste precious resources; almost any industry can grow if given sufficient protection, but some will not endure when their tariffs end. Next, one must determine how large a tariff is required to foster the development of a healthy infant. Excessive protection will encourage too much expansion, and the protected industry will contract when the tariff is removed. Finally, one must decide if the gains are worth the costs. The use of tariffs, even temporarily, will reduce world output during the transition and may even reduce real income in the country applying them. These direct and certain losses must be weighed against the distant and uncertain gains promised by protection.

Transitional protection also poses huge practical problems. Few industries will readily concede that they have grown up. During their adolescence, moreover, they will have acquired influential spokesmen in government because they have become important to the national or regional economy. It will then be difficult to strip them of their tariffs and expose them to the competition they grew up to face. Finally, some governments seem to believe that tariffs can *create* new industries; they restrict imports even when skilled labor, raw materials, and capital are too scarce to allow industrial development.

In brief, occasions that justify transitional protection may be quite rare, and an indiscriminate application of the transitional arguments by countries in the process of development may do great damage. As with most of the other tariff arguments, there may be better ways to reach an objective—ways that do not sacrifice efficiency or invite retaliation.

Summary

The structure and benefits of foreign trade both derive from the uneven international distribution of natural and man-made resources. Each country's endowment of land, minerals, skills, and machinery equips it to perform certain tasks more efficiently than others. Free trade allows a country to do the work it does best, then to trade the products of its most efficient industries for those that other countries make more economically. Trade is based on comparative advantage, not absolute advantage. Adjustments in wage rates (or in exchange rates) compensate for differences in over-all efficiency, allowing each country to adapt its production to its own resource endowment. The price system supplies the incentives to efficient specialization, and when wage rates are flexible, can also make the over-all cost-price adjustments needed to offset differences in absolute efficiency.

From the standpoint of the world as a whole, free trade is best. It works to maximize global output and is, therefore, a substitute for factor movements. One country, by contrast, may be able to improve its own position by restricting imports—by using a protective tariff or other trade controls to swing the terms of trade in its favor. But a tariff that can redistribute world income will also reduce it and is that much more harmful to other countries. There are similar objections to most of the other arguments for protective tariffs—for tariffs to alter the domestic income distribution and to raise employment. There are serious practical objections to the use of tariffs for stimulating economic growth in the less-developed countries.

3

PROBLEMS IN TRADE POLICY

Tariff Theory and Tariff History

At one time or another, every tariff argument has been used to justify high
import duties; some of them have also been invoked by those who advocate
free trade. Modern tariff history, then, is also the history of tariff theory, and
shows how economic theory affects public policy.

31

DIVERGENT TARIFF TRENDS: 1815–1860

During the first half of the nineteenth century, the infant-industries approach enjoyed a vogue in the United States. The country had just started its industrial development and sought to shelter its young manufactures from foreign competition. At about the same time, the distributional approach was used in Britain with opposite intent—to reduce existing tariffs. Even as the United States was moving toward protection, Britain was moving toward free trade.

The United States had taxed imports from its very birth as a nation. But its early tariffs, though protective in effect, were actually designed to raise money for the federal government. In those days, there was no income tax. The government relied on excise levies to finance its spending, and tariffs were the most important of these levies. A tax on imports was very easy to collect; one had merely to police the ports and coastline. It would have been still easier to tax the country's major exports—cotton and tobacco—but the southern states which grew and sold these products had insisted that the Constitution prohibit export duties. These states feared that the federal government, dominated by the more populous North, would seek to pay its way by taxing southern produce.

By 1815 there was strong support for a new tariff law fashioned to protect the young manufactures of New England and the Middle Atlantic states. The protracted war between Britain and Napoleonic France had disrupted the usual channels of trade, and Jefferson's Embargo, designed to prevent the impressment of American seamen by forbidding them to go to sea, had cut this country off from British textiles and hardware. The wars and embargo were equivalent to *prohibitive* tariffs on imported manufactures. They gave domestic industry an unrivaled opportunity. But with the coming of peace and the resumption of trade, British goods began again to cross the Atlantic, and American manufactures lost ground. Despite the opposition of the South, which naturally preferred to import cheaper foreign products, Congress levied higher duties on woolens and cottons (the Tariff Act of 1816) and placed higher taxes on imported glass, iron, and cutlery (the Tariff Act of 1824).

The North-South controversy over tariff legislation reached a bitter peak after 1828. In that year, the low tariff faction sought to outmaneuver its antagonists by amending a pending tariff bill. Southerners proposed high duties on raw wool and other crude materials, hoping that the northern manufacturers who used those materials would reject the entire tariff bill. But the stratagem failed and the bill became law (the Tariff Act of 1828). Its duties were the highest ever imposed prior to the Civil War, and it was promptly dubbed "The Tariff of Abominations." The tariff inspired South Carolina's "Ordinance of Nullification," which proclaimed a state's right to abrogate federal

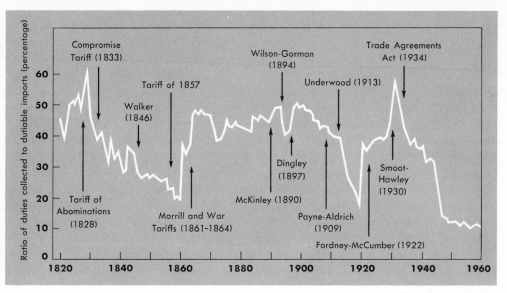

FIG. 11 Average U.S. rates of duty on dutiable imports. Legislation raising U.S. duties is usually reflected in an increase in the average on or after passage of the legislation. Legislation cutting U.S. duties is usually reflected in a decline in the average on or after passage. (Source: United States Department of Commerce, Bureau of the Census, *Historical Statistics of the United States* and *Statistical Abstract of the United States*, 1961.)

legislation, asserting that "the tariff law of 1828, and the amendment to the same of 1832, are null and void and no law, nor binding upon this State, its officers and citizens." But this first overt challenge to federal power met firm resistance from President Andrew Jackson, and the furor died down with passage of a compromise tariff in 1833.

In the 1840's the federal budget developed an embarrassing surplus and the Secretary of the Treasury proposed to reduce revenue by reducing tariffs. The average rate of duty on dutiable imports was brought down toward 26 per cent (see Fig. 11). Protective duties were cut sharply in 1846 and, again, in 1857. But the United States was still out of step with Western Europe, which was moving much closer to free trade.

The free-trade movement started in Great Britain as part of a broader assault on the powers of the aristocracy. It sought to end the political hegemony of the rural gentry, who were the chief beneficiaries of the Corn Laws—the tariffs on imported grain. As in the United States, therefore, tariff policy was entangled in broad constitutional questions, including the issue of parliamentary reform. The free-trade movement was also an offshoot of the attack on *mercantilism*—on state controls over trade and industry. The leaders of the movement owed a deep intellectual debt to Adam Smith, who had made the *allocative* case for free trade a full 50 years before the debates on the Corn Laws:

> What is prudence in the conduct of every private family, can scarce be folly in that of a great kingdom. If a foreign country can supply us with a

commodity cheaper than we ourselves can make it, better buy it of them with some part of the produce of our own industry, employed in a way in which we have some advantage. The general industry of the country, being always in proportion to the capital which employs it, will not thereby be diminished . . . but only left to find out the way in which it can be employed with the greatest advantage. It is certainly not employed to the greatest advantage, when it is thus directed toward an object which it can buy cheaper than it can make.

They were also indebted to David Ricardo and other disciples of Adam Smith who made the *distributive* case against the tax on grain. They contended that the Corn Laws were doubly injurious to the wage-earner. First, they said, tariffs raise food prices, reducing the purchasing power of the worker's wage. Second, they said, tariffs increase land rents at the expense of business profit, and low profits mean less saving, less investment, and, therefore, less demand for labor.

Britain had actually started toward free trade before the Napoleonic Wars. William Pitt had lowered many duties in 1784 and cut back others in the Eden Treaty with France (1786). After the Napoleonic Wars, the Tory government abolished or reduced many duties on industrial raw materials. This change followed long agitation by the merchants of London, who had a vital stake in free trade. It was supported by Britain's manufacturers, since the tariffs raised their operating costs by increasing the prices of raw materials. The reduction was not opposed by the gentry because they did not grow the materials involved. But during the next decade, attention shifted to the tax on grain—a much more explosive issue. In 1842 the Tory government of Sir Robert Peel successfully defeated a parliamentary motion to repeal the Corn Laws. The Tories took the side of the gentry. But the Irish potato famine of 1845–1846 forced Peel to allow larger grain imports so as to relieve the food shortage. He suspended the Corn Laws in 1845 and split his own party in 1846 by asking permanent repeal in the House of Commons. The Whig governments that followed, led by William Gladstone, dismantled most of Britain's other tariffs in the 1850's and 1860's.

THE TRIUMPH AND DECLINE OF FREE TRADE: 1860–1914

In its next step toward free trade, Britain turned from legislation to diplomacy. The Cobden-Chevalier Treaty of 1860 pledged Britain and France to a reciprocal reduction of tariffs, including a reduction in the British tax on French wines. The French then wrote tariff treaties with other European countries and with the *Zollverein,* the German customs union organized under Prussian auspices to permit free trade within Germany. The *Zollverein* reduced its external tariffs in exchange for French concessions on German exports.

The commercial treaties of 1860–1870 were doubly important. First, they brought about new tariff cuts, enlarging world markets. Second, they *generalized* all the tariff reductions each country had already made. They included the *most-favored-nation* clause, a standard provision in commercial treaties under which each signatory grants the other all concessions given to third countries. Under this clause, France gave the *Zollverein* the concessions it had given England in the 1860 treaty. The *Zollverein* was not obliged to make concessions in return, but was bound to grant France every tariff cut it had given or would give to any other country.

The free-trade movement, however, was soon to be defeated by a new constellation of attitudes and circumstances. The 1870's witnessed a sharp change in Europe's colonial policies. Imperialist sentiment had been dormant for half a century; no major colonies were founded after the Napoleonic Wars, apart from French acquisitions in North Africa. But in the 1870's the European powers scrambled madly for tropical real estate. The partition of Africa began and was nearly finished in the two decades after 1870, and there was renewed rivalry in the Near East and Orient. A bellicose nationalism captured European politics and was soon manifest in measures to protect domestic industry, especially the sectors making armaments, and to obtain control over foreign raw materials.

At about this same time European agriculture experienced a decisive change of fortune. Railroads and steamships brought wheat from Russia, the United States, and other distant countries into competition with German and French grain. Even Germany began to import wheat as farm prices fell. During the decades in which they had exported grain, European farmers and landowners had favored free trade, just like their counterparts in the American South. When farm prices fell, the farmers changed their minds; and with this change, the balance of political power swung toward protection. In Germany and France alike, a new coalition of young industry and injured agriculture reversed the trend in European tariff policy.

The tide turned in Germany in 1879. Six years earlier, Bismarck had abolished the tariff on iron and announced that tariffs on iron products would end in 1877. But he had over-reached himself. The Junkers of the east and farmers of the south united to support the beleaguered manufacturers of the Ruhr and Rhineland. Bismarck backtracked and in 1879 brought forward a new tariff affording substantial protection to industry and agriculture.

This new turn toward higher tariffs was defended by invoking the infant industries argument. That argument, indeed, was given its most elaborate formulation by a German, Friedrich List, who had lived in the United States and was impressed by the rapid growth of its economy behind high tariff walls. He returned to Germany as a passionate advocate of infant industries protection for his native country. His book, *The Closed Commercial State,* identified national power with industrial strength. List conceded that free trade was best from a cosmopolitan standpoint, but drew a sharp contrast between the allocative arguments and the national interest. No nation, he said, could afford to heed the cosmopolitan appeal until it had developed its own industries, for only then could every country take its rightful gains from the international division of labor. List's basic point was much like one I made earlier: Comparative advantage has a time-dimension, and the pattern of trade will reflect the *sequence* of national development. But List went much too far, arguing that countries can only prosper if they export manufactures, import foodstuffs, and consume tropical products. Denmark, Australia, and New Zealand give the lie to this assertion; they export farm products yet have higher living standards than most industrial countries. Unfortunately, List's argument won the day and survives to bedevil economic planning in the less-developed countries of our own era. Many of them hanker after massive industries although they might make much better use of their resources. They confuse steel mills and oil refineries with prosperity and national identity.

France followed Germany in 1892. Another coalition of industry and agriculture reversed the low-tariff policies of Napoleon III and enacted the famous Méline Tariff to promote industrial development. The French economy grew rapidly after 1890, but the Méline Tariff cannot take much credit. Indeed, it may have hindered growth in the iron and steel industry, as it levied a high tax on coal, raising the costs of the French iron manufacturers.

The resurgence of protectionism in the 1890's was followed by a period of tariff warfare, especially among Germany, Russia, and Italy. In 1902 Germany actually raised its tariff so as to obtain more leeway for bargaining, and peppered its tariff schedule with trivial distinctions so as to differentiate the exports of one country from those of another. To distinguish Swiss from Danish cattle, for example, the 1902 tariff had a separate category applying to "brown or dappled cows reared at a level or at least 300 metres above sea level and passing at least one month in every summer at an altitude of at least 800 metres." Hence, a German rate reduction applying to Danish cattle would not automatically accrue to Switzerland under the *most-favored-nation* clause.

American tariffs did not come down as fast or as far as European tariffs in the middle third of the nineteenth century. After 1860, moreover, they went up further. In 1861 Congress passed the Morrill Tariff Act, giving new protection to the iron and steel industry; and in 1862 and 1864, approved a sweeping increase in most other duties. These higher rates were voted to deny foreigners an unfair advantage over U.S. producers, not to give Americans additional protection; Congress imposed heavy excise taxes on many domestic products to finance the Civil War, and the new import tariffs were meant to offset them. When the war ended, however, the domestic excise taxes were allowed to lapse as government spending declined, but the import duties were not dismantled. They then came to exercise a severe protective effect. American tariffs reached a post-war peak during the McKinley administration (the Tariff Act of 1890). They came down again in 1894, when control of Congress passed briefly to the Democrats and Grover Cleveland occupied the White House. But a Republican Congress raised them to a new peak in the Tariff Act of 1897.

After 1900 the Republican party seemed to edge away from extreme protectionism. Its 1908 platform declared that "the true principle of protection is best maintained by the imposition of such duties as would equalize the difference between the cost of production at home and abroad, together with a reasonable degree of profit." This formula looked thoroughly reasonable and was reflected in the Tariff Act of 1909, which cut some duties slightly. But what you have already learned about foreign trade should show you that this "scientific" formula really provides extravagant protection. Differences in costs are the basis for trade, and a tariff set to offset cost differences will therefore prohibit trade, save for flows of tropical products and raw materials not produced domestically. If differences in national costs of production are offset by a tariff, transport costs will usually suffice to bar imports of foreign manufactures.

COLLAPSE AND RECONSTRUCTION: 1914-1939

On the eve of the First World War, the United States made a major tariff change. The Wilson administration reduced the tariff drastically in 1913 and added several major items to the "free list," including iron, coal, raw wool, lumber, and newsprint. But the end of the World War brought new pressure for protection here and in other countries.

The war and peace settlements wrecked the international financial system. They disrupted established trade patterns and rearranged capital flows. They burdened the financial system with several heavy layers of debt and large debt-service payments. Many Allied governments had borrowed in the United States to finance their purchases of war materiel. Then, the peace treaties levied reparations debts on the defeated nations. The old Austrian Empire was chopped up into a half-dozen states—Czechoslovakia, Hungary, and the rest—each obliged to make its separate way in world markets. Europe's tariff frontiers were lengthened by some 12,000 miles. Some of the victors suffered as much as the vanquished. Britain had been forced to sell many of its foreign assets to finance its war effort, foregoing the investment income that had served to offset a decline in its major export industries before 1914.

To make matters worse, many American industries had expanded rapidly during the war, and feared intense competition with the end of hostilities. This was the case with the chemicals industry, and it was the first to win extra protection after the war. The same thing happened in agriculture, here and in other countries. Encouraged to expand production during the war, farmers confronted ruinous competition afterward and faced adverse terms of trade throughout the 1920's. Rampant inflation compounded the general disorder. In 1923 a German housewife had to carry her money to market in a shopping bag, and could carry her groceries home in a change purse.

One by one, governments levied new tariffs. Some imposed outright import quotas. The new nations of Central Europe were among the first, but they were not alone. Germany imposed a new agricultural tariff in 1925. The countries of Latin America applied tariffs and quotas much more freely than they had before the war. And Britain finally lapsed from free trade in 1919, levied additional tariffs in 1921, and succumbed to systematic protection in 1931, amidst a general economic crisis.

The United States should have lowered its tariffs so that the outside world might earn more dollars to service its debts. Instead, Congress voted higher duties in 1922, during the first post-war depression. The Fordney-McCumber Tariff of 1922 was designed to aid the farmers, but also helped the chemicals industry and other "war babies."

The trend toward agricultural protection and quantitative trade controls continued in the second half of the 1920's. It was capped by our own Hawley-Smoot Tariff of 1930, once called the "Holy Smoke Tariff" by an undergraduate with more perception than memory. Congress began hearings on tariff reform in January 1929, again intent on helping the farmers. But then the stock market collapsed and the economy began its sickening slide toward the Great Depression. One industry after another clamored for increased protection to stimulate employment, and when the new tariff bill was laid before Congress, an orgy of logrolling began. Congressmen traded votes with one another, seeking higher tariffs for their own constituents. When it was all over, the United States had the highest tariff in its history and other countries felt compelled to restrict imports from the United States. The Hawley-Smoot Tariff dashed all hopes for global recovery through expanded trade—hopes that had been fostered by earlier efforts to achieve a tariff truce.

The early 1930's gave birth to a new generation of trade controls. Struggling to prevent the spread of the depression, country after country cracked down on imports with new tariffs and other restrictions. Each one sought to stimulate domestic production by protecting local business against foreign competition. Each one, in turn, frustrated its neighbor's efforts to do the same thing; a fall in one country's imports meant a fall in another's exports. And after Great Britain had devalued the pound in 1931 and the United States had devalued the dollar in 1934, France and other European countries began to use import controls to defend their currencies.

Foreign trade actually lagged behind production in the slow recovery from the Great Depression. It was, indeed, a drag rather than a stimulant to faster expansion. In 1928 world imports totaled $60.1 billion; in 1938, they were a mere $24.6 billion—less than half the pre-depression level.

In the United States the trough in employment and production came in 1933. The peak in U.S. tariffs had come in 1932. Thereafter, however, our import duties started to decline. A part of this reduction was caused by the increase in prices after 1932. Many U.S. tariffs are *specific* duties, fixed in cents per pound, dollars per dozen, and so on. When prices fall, the *ad valorem* (percentage) equivalents of these duties rise; when prices rise, the equivalents decline. A 10¢ tariff on a $1.00 product works out to 10 per cent; if the price falls to 50¢, the duty works out to 20 per cent; and if the price rises to $2.00, the duty works out to 5 per cent.

But the decline was also caused by a major turnabout in U.S. tariff policy. Casting about for ways to increase employment, the Roosevelt administration finally turned to the world market, launching a campaign to reduce trade barriers and expand U.S. exports. In 1934 President Roosevelt asked Congress for power to negotiate trade agreements cutting U.S. tariffs by as much as half in return for equivalent concessions by other countries. The president told Congress:

> A resumption of international trade cannot but improve the general situation of other countries, and thus increase their purchasing power. Let us well remember that this in turn spells increased opportunity for American sales. . . . Legislation such as this is an essential step in the program of national economic recovery which the Congress has elaborated during this past year.

He promised that the U.S. tariff cuts would not injure American producers—that he would not open American markets to competitive imports. In effect, he foreswore the allocative gains from trade, looking instead for effects on employment. He apparently planned to bargain off our *surplus* protection—rates that could be cut without attracting imports.

Congress gave the president the powers he wanted; and the United States negotiated 31 trade agreements with other governments from 1934 through 1945. In each case, the United States generalized its own concessions to most of the other trading countries under the *most-favored-nation* clause. The Trade Agreements Program was much like the network of trade treaties that spread out from France following the Cobden-Chevalier Treaty of 1860. Unlike that treaty system, however, it did not bring the nations close to free trade. The average U.S. tariff in 1939 was just below what it had been 10 years earlier, on the eve of the Hawley-Smoot debacle. Yet the Trade Agreements Program did help to arrest the worldwide tariff increase that had been choking world trade. It also held U.S. tariffs down during and after the Second World War, whereas, after every other major war, tariffs had risen substantially. This restraint was extremely impressive, since the inflation of the 1940's greatly reduced the *ad valorem* value of U.S. specific duties. By 1945, then, the average American tariff was as low as it had been in 1919.

The Multilateral Approach to Trade Policy

The Second World War damaged world trade even more than the Great Depression. Most of the belligerents imposed strict *exchange controls* to prevent their citizens from spending foreign currencies; they sought to reserve their precious foreign earnings for purchasing war materiel and food. Many countries carried their controls into the post-war period in order to save scarce foreign currency for their reconstruction programs.

Very early in the war, however, experts began drawing plans to liberalize trade and payments in the post-war period. Even before the shooting stopped, the Allied governments established two new financial institutions—the International Monetary Fund (IMF) and the International Bank for Reconstruction and Development (IBRD)—to revive and sustain the payments system and encourage flows of long-term capital. They also planned to promote a fast recovery of world trade by relaxing the complex controls that had slowed recovery in the 1930's and strangled trade during the war.

The experts found serious flaws in the Trade Agreements Program. During the pre-war negotiations, many governments had withheld tariff concessions from the United States to save some of their limited bargaining power for negotiations with other countries. The wartime planners consequently urged a *multilateral* agreement rather than a new set of country-by-country bargains. Each government might then weigh all it had won—the concessions it had obtained directly in return for its own and those it had obtained indirectly through the *most-favored-nation* clause. The American experts likewise worried about the import quotas, payments agreements, and other trade controls that had been used abroad in lieu of tariffs. Quotas frustrate the price mechanism by barring imports no matter how cheap. Tariffs handicap the foreigner but do not freeze trade patterns or prevent price changes from affecting resource allocation. Furthermore, quotas were sometimes used abroad to nullify negotiated tariff cuts; some countries had imposed import quotas after they had cut their duties. The United States consequently sought a comprehensive agreement on commercial policy, not just a new tariff treaty.

The new U.S. trade policy found its first expression in wartime agreements between the United States and Great Britain—in the Atlantic Charter and Lend-Lease Agreement. The new policy was then embodied in a charter for an International Trade Organization (ITO) to be affiliated with the United Nations. But the ITO never came into being. Its charter was too long and complicated, and was perforated by exceptions and qualifications. It antagonized opponents of international cooperation, who charged that the ITO would meddle with domestic economic policies. It antagonized the advocates of cooperation, who complained that the exceptions and qualifications had swamped the principles, and that no one would be bound to obey the rules.

In 1947, however, the major governments were able to agree on interim rules for trade policy and began a series of conferences to reduce tariffs and dismantle other barriers. This interim arrangement has survived and is known as the General Agreement on Tariffs and Trade (GATT). The GATT is a simple document compared to the ITO charter; it does not seek to deal with every issue or to anticipate every contingency. The heart of the GATT is a *most-favored-nation* clause which provides that every tariff bargain made at GATT meetings shall be extended to all member countries. This is how the system works: At each GATT conference, national negotiators meet in pairs to swap tariff cuts in which they have special interest. Thus, American and British representatives may sit down to exchange concessions on cars and woolens, even as British and French representatives are bargaining on pharmaceuticals and wines, and the Americans and French are bargaining on office machinery and perfumes. When all the separate bargains are complete, they are listed in a single schedule and applied to every member country. This combination of bilateral and multilateral negotiations seems cumbersome, but has had great advantages. Each government negotiates with the others that will gain most from its proposed concessions, thereby securing the largest foreign concessions in return for its own. At the same time, every government can keep track of the benefits it will obtain from all other countries and appraise its global bargaining position as the negotiations proceed.

The GATT commercial code outlaws discriminatory tariffs and prohibits the use of import quotas except by countries suffering from balance-of-payments problems or by those imposing similar quotas on domestic production—on farm products, for example. It allows the less-developed countries to protect their infant industries, but subjects them to regular GATT review. The GATT provides machinery to resolve disputes arising from trade policy. During the last few years, for example, it has been disentangling the problems raised by the creation of the European Economic Community, or Common Market. The formation of the Common Market poses a host of problems for outsiders, including the United States, and GATT members have asked the European countries to adjust their policies to minimize damage and dislocation.

OBSTACLES TO TARIFF BARGAINING

In 1945 Congress passed another Trade Agreements Act, giving the president new powers to reduce American tariffs in international bargaining. The United States then took part in several GATT conferences. In 1950–1951, for example, the United States made concessions to 22 countries covering a third of its dutiable imports from those countries. To see how these GATT meetings affected U.S. tariff rates, compare the last two columns in Table 2; duties declined in every major category, and some rates fell substantially.

American imports did not respond to these tariff cuts until other countries had made good the damage done by war and could raise their exports.

TABLE 2

Tariff Reductions Since 1934, by Commodity Class
(Duties collected as a percentage of 1952 dutiable imports)

Commodity Class	1934	1945	1953
All dutiable imports	24.4	17.9	12.2
Chemicals, oils, and paints	25.1	20.0	12.4
Earthenware and glassware	40.6	36.7	24.7
Metals and metal products	23.7	18.9	12.1
Wood and wood products	10.9	7.5	4.7
Sugar and molasses	25.8	13.5	9.4
Tobacco and tobacco products	45.6	34.7	20.3
Agricultural products	16.2	12.5	9.4
Spirits, wines, and other beverages	81.4	41.6	23.1
Cotton products	36.8	30.0	21.8
Flax, hemp, and jute	12.2	9.0	5.2
Wool and wool products	36.7	30.2	22.4
Silk products	58.8	52.7	31.0
Synthetic-fiber textiles	32.8	31.0	17.7
Pulp, paper, and books	20.4	15.2	9.4
Sundries	31.8	26.5	19.1

Source: United States Tariff Commission, "Effect of Trade Agreement Concessions on United States Tariff Levels," 1954.

Recently, however, dutiable imports have been growing faster than duty-free imports, and there has been a considerable rise in manufactured imports, due partly to post-war tariff cuts.

The early post-war cuts were the ones that mattered most. In fact, U.S. tariffs hardly changed between the 1950–1951 GATT negotiations and the 1960–1961 bargaining with the Common Market. American negotiators could not make large tariff reductions in the 1950's, as Congress had hobbled them by amending the Trade Agreements Act.

When President Roosevelt first asked for authority to reduce U.S. tariffs, he promised that no injury would befall American industry. When President Truman requested additional tariff-cutting powers in 1945, he renewed this promise. But these assurances did not satisfy Congress, and when the Trade Agreements Act had to be renewed again in 1947, the president promulgated formal procedures to redress injury. He asked the Tariff Commission, a six-man board appointed by the president, to hear petitions brought by industries claiming injury from import competition. When it found evidence of injury, the Commission was to recommend increased tariffs or other import restrictions. The president reserved the right to set aside these recommendations, but had put himself on the defensive, since he would henceforth have to justify refusing protection.

Protectionist sentiment grew stronger still in the early 1950's. With the reconstruction of war-damaged industries abroad, American industry began to meet competition from Western Europe and Japan. Labor unions were beginning to worry about low-wage foreign labor. And some southern congressmen had abandoned their historic opposition to high tariffs; as the South experienced industrial development, they rediscovered the infant-industries argument. In 1951 Congress wrote an *escape clause* into the Trade Agreements Act, formalizing the procedures established in 1947 and listing the criteria to be used in appraising a complaint of injury:

> In arriving at a determination . . . the Tariff Commission, without excluding other factors, shall take into consideration a downward trend of production, employment, prices, profits, or wages in the domestic industry concerned, or a decline in sales, an increase in imports, either actual or relative to domestic production, a higher or growing inventory, or a decline in the proportion of the domestic market supplied by domestic producers.

Notice that an increase in imports was to be regarded as a *measure* of injury, as well as a cause, and that it did not have to be an absolute increase. A company could ask for higher tariffs if its sales increased but imports increased faster.

In 1955 and 1958, Congress broadened the escape clause and made it more difficult for the president to reject Tariff Commission recommendations. It also wrote a National Security Amendment into the law:

> . . . The President shall . . . give consideration to domestic production needed for projected national defense requirements, . . . existing and anticipated availabilities of the human resources, products, raw materials, and other supplies and services essential to the national defense, and the requirements of growth in such . . . supplies and services including the investment, exploration, and development necessary to assure such growth, . . . and shall take into consideration the impact of foreign competition on the economic welfare of individual domestic industries . . . in determining whether such weakening of our internal economy may impair the national security.

This amendment made very little sense. Economists have always conceded the need to protect industries required for defense production. Thus, Adam Smith supported Britain's *Navigation Acts,* because "the defense of Great Britain . . . depends very much upon the number of its sailors and shipping." In our day, however, a nation's security depends on the arsenal of weapons built up before hostilities have started. This country's power to combat aggression is not enhanced by tariffs protecting domestic manufacturers of watches, lead and zinc miners, or the oil industry, and sustaining their skills for use in war production the day after someone has dropped the bomb.

The sweeping phrases of the National Security Amendment really serve a more general protective purpose—to erect another barrier against import competition. The amendment, incidentally, has been invoked only once—to place quotas on imports of petroleum, including residual fuel oil used for heating. These import quotas were ostensibly designed to reward exploration for new petroleum deposits, but also protected the depressed soft-coal industry which has been injured by the changeover from coal to fuel oil in industrial and household heating.

The escape clause and National Security Amendment gave relief from injury after it had happened. Another clause in the Trade Agreements Act was meant to forestall injury. In 1948 Congress enacted a *peril-point* provision which directed the president to list the products on which he planned to make concessions at GATT meetings so that the Tariff Commission might decide what duties are needed to prevent injury. The president could still cut a tariff far below its "peril point," but was obliged to give his reasons in a special message to Congress.

The escape clause, National Security Amendment, and peril-point provision did not turn the tide of U.S. tariff policies. But they prevented further tariff cuts. Furthermore, some 15 duties were raised pursuant to the escape clause, damaging U.S. relations with friendly countries. Switzerland was injured and offended by an increase in the U.S. watch tariff. Belgium expressed serious doubts about our sincerity in tariff bargaining, when, just after making a major agreement with the European Common Market, the United States applied new tariffs to Wilton carpets, an important Belgian export. The escape clause and National Security Amendment also warned other countries that U.S. tariff concessions might be snatched away at any moment if exploited too successfully. Finally, the peril-point provision sometimes caused foreigners to withhold concessions from the United States because the United States could not reply in kind. In 1960-1961, the European Common Market proposed a 20 per cent reduction in its common external tariff if the United States would make a similar reduction. When it became apparent that the American negotiators could not make so broad a cut because of the peril-point provision, the Europeans pared down their offer.

THE EUROPEAN INITIATIVE

Every two years or so in the 1950's, the White House had to ask for another renewal of the Trade Agreements Act. Congress granted the renewal, but drilled new loopholes into the law. Each time, a parade of industry spokesmen appeared before congressional committees to demand increased protection and denounce low tariffs as the source of all their woes. After much maneuvering, the administration purchased renewal of its bargaining authority by agreeing to amendments restricting the president's freedom of action and providing better ways to redress injury.

Yet the advocates of liberal trade policies were not dissatisfied with this ritual. They argued that tariffs are not the major barriers to trade; quotas and limitations on the interconvertibility of foreign currencies do much more damage. They also said that few foreign countries could give us much in tariff bargaining, for their markets were too small. This was an accurate description of the situation in the early 1950's. But even as the United States marked time, things were happening in Europe to undermine these premises. The European governments were making dramatic decisions that would change the balance of advantage in bargaining. Today, most experts would agree, the United States has far more to gain than lose from new negotiations.

At the close of the Second World War, the United States began an unprecedented financial effort to aid the reconstruction of Western Europe. This was the Marshall Plan. At the same time, it urged the Europeans to combine their resources and realize an age-old dream—a United States of Europe. Washington was concerned to strengthen Europe against the Soviet threat and, as urgently, to bind Germany into a democratic federation so that it might never again destroy the peace.

At first, the Europeans started to integrate one industry at a time—the sector-by-sector approach to unification. They established a European Coal and Steel Community, making for free trade in coal and steel and creating a supranational High Authority with power to regulate pricing policies and commercial practices. Then the Europeans changed their tactics. In the mid-1950's they began to work for a full *customs union* of 6 continental countries—France, Germany, Italy, the Netherlands, Belgium, and Luxembourg. In 1957 these 6 countries signed the Treaty of Rome, establishing the European Economic Community (EEC), or Common Market. They agreed to eliminate all barriers to trade among themselves and to surround themselves with a common external tariff—a set of duties constructed by averaging their separate national tariffs. They also agreed to "harmonize" domestic policies, including farm policies, to lift restrictions on the movement of men and money inside Europe, and to plan for political unification. At the start, the EEC moved slowly toward its aim. But it has revised its timetable, speeding up the process of economic integration.

For many Europeans, political unification is the most important objective of the Treaty of Rome. Washington apparently feels the same way. But the member countries also expect to reap great economic gains by eliminating tariffs within Europe and coordinating other economic policies. First, they expect to intensify competition—thereby fostering a more efficient use of European resources and a better allocation of economic tasks. Second, they expect to capture the economies of scale usually associated with large markets. The 6 EEC members have a combined population of about 170 million and a gross regional product approaching $200 billion. It is about as populous as the United States and a third as wealthy.

A year after signing the Treaty of Rome, the European governments took another major step. They made their currencies convertible, removing the remaining justification for discrimination against American goods. Once francs, marks, and pounds could be used to buy dollars, no country could require that its citizens buy European goods to conserve dollar earnings. The Europeans consequently ended most of their remaining import quotas.

The creation of the European Common Market and the restoration of convertibility have left tariffs as the major barriers to trade. Tariff policy has begun to matter once again. Moreover, the formation of the Common Market has created a constellation of countries and markets large enough to bargain with the United States. And all these developments have helped to foster rapid economic growth in Europe, creating stunning opportunities for American industry. There has been a heavy flow of private American capital to Western Europe, as hundreds of American corporations have built factories there. Many American industries already manufacture more abroad than they export from their plants in the United States. Overseas production has grown much more rapidly than United States exports. The exports listed in Table 3 are just 10 per cent larger than they were in 1957; the overseas production in that table is 40 per cent larger.

But the European Economic Community presents a challenge to American trade policy as well as a great opportunity. Although the Common Market's tariff schedule may not be more restrictive than the separate national tariffs from which it was built, Europe's new commercial arrangements can damage trade patterns severely. Before the creation of the Common Market, American, German, and Italian goods paid the same duties when they entered France. Soon, German and Italian products will not pay any duty, and American products will still be taxed. The EEC discriminates against outsiders. And as U.S. firms invest in Europe in order to leap over the common tariff, in-

TABLE 3

U.S. Exports of Selected Manufactures and Production by U.S. Companies Abroad, 1961 (Millions of dollars)

Product Class	U.S. Exports	Production Abroad
Paper and allied products	453	1,310
Chemicals	1,709	3,975
Rubber products	330	1,215
Non-electrical machinery	3,595	2,738
Electrical machinery	867	2,470
Transportation equipment	1,281*	6,000
All items	8,235	17,705

*Excluding civilian aircraft.
Source: United States Department of Commerce, *Survey of Current Business*, September, 1962.

vestment and employment in the United States may also be reduced—or may grow more slowly than they would if there were no Common Market.

Faced with this challenge to our own and other countries' trade, the Kennedy administration has obtained new trade legislation. The Trade Expansion Act of 1962 empowers the president to cut U.S. tariffs once again, but differently this time. Heretofore, the United States has bargained on a rate-by-rate, product-by-product basis. Henceforth, it will make more sweeping agreements. It will be able to cut *all* its tariffs in half, in return for similar "across the board" reductions by other countries. It will also be able to eliminate its tariffs on products that are mainly made in the Common Market and the United States.

The Trade Expansion Act also portends a fundamental change in technique. It modifies the basic "no injury" rule that has hobbled United States negotiators and impaired the logic of U.S. tariff policy. A country exports so that it can import. Yet the old Trade Agreements Acts were chiefly concerned to increase United States exports. They looked on additional imports as the price we had to pay to widen our export markets—and one this country would not pay if increased imports damaged domestic industry. The new law begins by redefining injury. Henceforth, the Tariff Commission will require evidence that men and machines have been idled by import competition, not merely that prices have fallen or that imports have grown faster than domestic output. Next, the law provides new ways to cope with injury. Instead of imposing additional import restrictions, the president may authorize direct aid—extended unemployment compensation and retraining for workers, tax benefits and loans for employers to help them diversify or modernize their plants. Thus, the new law seeks to capture the allocative gains from trade by fostering shifts in resource use, rather than renouncing those gains by restricting imports and subsidizing inefficient industries.

The Trade Expansion Act cannot solve all the problems of trade policy. It may be wholly impotent to expand world trade in agricultural commodities. For many years, the United States has used import quotas on cotton, wheat, dairy products, and other major staples. These quotas prop up our own high support prices; if imports could enter the United States without limit, the government would be hard pressed to keep domestic farm prices above world levels. Now the EEC has decided to use much the same system, though it will use variable import levies—taxes that move up and down to align world and domestic prices. These new European restrictions will damage the United States. You doubtless think of the United States as a manufacturer. But farm products bulk large in our total exports. The United States is the world's largest exporter of cotton, wheat, and tobacco. It must preserve its markets for these crops in the other industrial countries, especially in Western Europe.

For that matter, freer trade in farm products would be beneficial to Western Europe. The Common Market countries are short of labor and can ill-afford to keep men on the land. Yet farm prices are a sensitive political issue everywhere, and few experts believe that the Trade Expansion Act will bring down the barriers to agricultural trade.

There is even danger that squabbles over agriculture may prevent bargaining on manufactured goods, and this would be a major setback for the international economy. Freer trade between Western Europe and the United States would improve resource allocation within the industrial world and could provide the less-developed countries with a new stimulus to growth. Our own tariffs are still high enough to restrict world trade, and there are major differences between the U.S. tariff schedule and that of the Common Market, so that the two can bargain with mutual benefit. The Common Market tariffs on chemicals, machinery, and vehicles are higher than the corresponding U.S. tariffs (see Table 4). But U.S. duties on textiles and apparel, ceramics and glassware, optical equipment, and watches are higher than those of the EEC.

Tariff reduction will do damage to several industries. But continued protection may not be much help to them over the long run. Many of the industries most apt to be affected by trade liberalization have been limping along. even with high tariffs. A recent study of employment in protected industries shows that:

> . . . the heavily protected, import-competing industries are not only predominantly declining, but they are declining more than the less protected, import-competing industries.[1]

Another study indicates that the problem of adjustment to increased imports will not be very large.[2] A $1 billion increase in dutiable imports spread across all industries and displacing $1 billion of domestic production would decrease employment in many industries:

Gross *decrease* in the import-competing industries	63,000 man-years
Gross *decrease* in other industries	52,000 man-years
Gross *decrease* in all industries	115,000 man-years

But these calculations do not allow for the increase in United States exports that would follow the reduction of other countries' tariffs nor for the increase

[1] Beatrice N. Vaccara, *Employment and Output in Protected Manufacturing Industries* (Washington, D.C.: The Brookings Institution, 1960), p. 68.

[2] The data that follow are taken from Walter S. Salant and Beatrice N. Vaccara, *Import Liberalization and Employment* (Washington, D.C.: The Brookings Institution, 1961), p. 215. They relate to a $1 billion increase of imports at 1953 prices and to the median data for 72 import-competing industries.

TABLE 4

U.S. and Common Market Tariffs on Industrial Products (Percentage equivalents weighted by 1960 imports; rates in force prior to the 1961 GATT negotiations)

Commodity Class	United States	Common Market
Mineral products	3.0	2.4
Chemicals and allied products	6.9	13.0
Plastics and plastic products	2.7	10.0
Leather and leather products	6.5	2.9
Wood and wood products	6.0	6.1
Pulp, paper, and paper products	0.8	7.9
Textile fibers, textiles, and textile products	19.0	7.5
Stone, ceramic, and glass products	25.8	15.0
Base metals and metal products	7.4	5.9
Machinery and mechanical appliances	10.9	13.8
Vehicles, aircraft, and other transport equipment	10.9	17.5
Optical, photographic and scientific instruments, watches and clocks	25.3	15.9

Source: Committee for Economic Development, *A New Trade Policy for the United States,* 1962.

that would occur merely because foreigners were earning more dollars and were willing to spend them on our exports. Notice, further, that part of the gross decrease in employment would be very widely diffused, not wholly concentrated in the import-competing industries. This is because every firm buys materials and services from others.

Admittedly, much of the job-loss due to larger imports would focus on a few firms and communities, many of them in deep trouble now on account of changes in tastes and technology. In 14 out of 72 industries, a $50 million increase in imports would suffice to double or more than double the gross separation rate (quits and layoffs). Finally, the trade adjustment program will not work unless the American economy is growing. Companies will not diversify production if they lack new markets. Workers will not benefit from retraining if there are no new jobs. European experience shows that the adjustment to import competition is easiest when aggregate demand is growing rapidly, so that new opportunities abound for those who lose their livelihood. If, indeed, there is any reason to insist that the American economy grow faster, it is because more rapid growth will permit an easier adjustment to disturbances—changes in tastes and technology and increased import competition. The pull of buoyant demand seems to be more effective in reshuffling resources than the sting of shrinking markets and high unemployment.

Summary

The tariff histories of Western Europe and the United States describe two similar cycles. Both histories reflect the influence of economic theory, industrial development, and international politics.

In Europe, tariffs started downward after the Napoleonic Wars, reaching their nadir after 1860. Britain led the way with a unilateral reduction; the continental countries followed suit, by way of tariff treaties. Tariffs moved up again after 1880, with the re-emergence of aggressive nationalism and the shift in political power caused by the shifts in agricultural trade. Trade restrictions became even more severe in the 1920's, and the global depression of the 1930's caused many countries to impose import quotas. The quantitative trade controls of the 1930's remained in force through the Second World War, but were gradually dismantled in the 1950's. Then, the Europeans began to cut their tariff barriers as well, but chiefly in respect to European trade, not on imports from the outside world. The European Economic Community, or Common Market, is the end-product of this trend. It will eliminate all trade barriers within Western Europe and facilitate the free flow of labor and capital.

In the United States, tariffs moved upward after the Napoleonic Wars, but came down briefly during the 1840's and 1850's, coincident with the repeal of the British Corn Laws. They moved up again during the Civil War, and did not decline until the eve of the First World War. Afterward, moreover, the U.S. tariff rose again; it hit its all-time high with the Hawley-Smoot Tariff Act of 1930. Then, in the 1930's, the United States negotiated tariff treaties with a great number of countries, and in the 1940's and 1950's participated in new tariff bargaining under the auspices of the General Agreement on Tariffs and Trade. The U.S. program lost momentum in the 1950's as Congress added three restrictive amendments to the Trade Agreements Act— the escape clause, the peril-point provision, and the National Security Amendment. In 1962, however, Congress passed new trade legislation as a response to the challenge of the EEC. The president is now empowered to reduce most U.S. tariffs and to assist the injured industries instead of having to curb imports when they harm American producers.

The coming decade is apt to witness a further reduction of tariffs among the industrial countries, with benefit to them and to the less-developed countries. But the special problems of trade in farm products are far from solution, and the new trade adjustment program will not help injured industries unless the American economy expands to furnish new job opportunities.

THE BALANCE OF PAYMENTS
AND FOREIGN-EXCHANGE MARKET

Balance-of-Payments Accounting

Thus far, you have studied the effects of foreign trade on resource allocation and on income distribution—always assuming that the stream of payments from one country to another is balanced by a stream of payments from the second to the first. This equality can be secured by wage-rate or exchange-rate changes. In Chapter 2, you will recall, American wage rates and prices

51

were at first so low that consumers in America and Britain both preferred to buy American coal but were indifferent as between American or British potatoes. Trade did not balance. Then, foreign demand for American coal raised America's wage rate until its potatoes became more expensive than British potatoes. A balanced flow of trade ensued. As a matter of actual fact, however, wage rates and prices may not respond smoothly to correct an imbalance in international payments. Wages and other costs may be very sticky. They may even move independently of demand conditions, *causing* a lopsided flow of payments. Furthermore, some international cash flows will not act on wage rates and prices so as to restore equilibrium; a demand for foreign securities, for example, will not change wage rates directly.

Under these circumstances, governments seeking to maintain fixed exchange rates may face serious monetary problems in their relations with the outside world. Economists sometimes describe these monetary problems as "transitional" or "short-run" phenomena that should not be allowed to divert our attention from the "real" flows—goods, services, and capital. But the "short-run" may drag on for a long time, and imperfections in the process of wage-rate, price, and exchange-rate adjustment may actually alter the "real" flows. If wage rates and exchange rates are rigid, a country may not be able to balance its international transactions at a satisfactory level of domestic employment or may have to forego economic growth. The recent condition of the United States *balance of payments,* the sum total of American transactions with foreigners, has discouraged the government from adopting financial policies to stimulate domestic growth.

As a preface to international monetary problems and policies, we will examine a group of transactions put together as a hypothetical *balance-of-payments* table for the United States. Then we will study several ways of balancing the cash flows that arise from these transactions.

A balance-of-payments table is designed to summarize a nation's total transactions with the outside world. It is usually divided into three sections:

The current account, which shows flows of goods and services;
The capital account, which shows lending and investment;
The cash account, which shows flows of cash and short-term credit that finance the current and capital transactions.

This three-way division is especially convenient for economic analysis. To see how a country's foreign trade affects income and employment, an economist has only to look at the current account. This account will show total foreign spending on current domestic output, for it will list the country's exports of domestic goods and services. It will also tabulate the country's spending on foreign goods and services and, therefore, its contribution to foreign income and employment. Notice, incidentally, that all our work in Chapter 2 dealt with the current account and assumed that current-account outlays (imports) were equal to current-account earnings (exports).

The capital and cash accounts show how foreign trade and payments affect wealth and debt. If American citizens acquire foreign stocks and bonds —claims on foreigners—they will earn income in the future, and when they sell their claims, can buy foreign goods and services. If, instead, American citizens borrow money from a foreign bank or sell securities to foreigners, they will have to make interest payments in the future, and when their debts become due, must sell more goods and services to foreigners.

Some foreign debts and claims are easily classified. The purchase of a permanent interest in a foreign corporation is a long-term capital transaction. The acquisition of a foreign bank deposit is a cash transaction. But how should a 3-month bank loan be classified? Such a loan is an earning asset, but is also akin to cash, for it will mature very quickly. How should a foreign purchase of a U.S. Treasury bill be classified? It is an earning asset for the foreigner, just like a bond or stock, but is a substitute for cash because it matures quite fast. Many foreign banks and governments invest their dollar holdings in short-term securities like Treasury bills, rather than holding them as idle bank deposits.

The dividing line between capital and cash is drawn so that claims and debts maturing in one year or less go into the cash account, and those that mature in more than a year (or have no fixed maturity) are put into the capital account. Like any arbitrary rule, this one leads to strange results. But we need some sort of rule so that the accounts will be consistent and permit comparisons through time.

Every international transaction will appear in 2 of the 3 accounts—or more than once in one account. This is because every transaction involves a transfer of goods, services, or securities against cash or a debt-instrument (an IOU or bank loan). Each one will be entered as a *debit* (with a minus sign) insofar as it enlarges the supply of goods and services available to Americans, adds to U.S. claims on foreigners, or reduces U.S. debts to foreigners. Each one will be entered as a *credit* (with a plus sign) insofar as it reduces the supply of goods and services, reduces U.S. claims on foreigners, or increases U.S. indebtedness. To illustrate, consider these five transactions:

1. *An American purchase of $280,000 worth of tin from Malaya, paid for with pounds sterling bought with dollars from a New York bank.*

A purchase of tin will appear on current account because it creates income abroad. It will appear as a *debit* there because it enlarges the supply of goods available to Americans. It is listed next to *commodity imports* in Table 5. The transfer of pounds sterling to pay for the tin will appear on cash account as a change in *U.S. holdings of foreign currencies.* It will be a *credit* there because it reduces American monetary claims on the outside world (U.S. holdings of pounds sterling). The American importer of tin will go to a New York bank, write a check for $280,000 (plus a small commission), and receive a *draft* for £100,000 drawn on his bank's balance at a London bank. The ratio of $280: £100 or $2.80: £1 is the exchange rate between the dollar and the pound sterling. Next, the American importer will pass the sterling draft over to the Malayan tin producer who will sell it to his bank in Singapore, obtaining the Malayan equivalent of £100,000. To complete the transaction, the bank in Singapore will forward the draft to London, where the bank on which the draft was drawn will deduct £100,000 from the sterling balance of the New York bank that issued it.

2. *An American sale of $300,000 worth of antibiotics to Venezuela, paid for with dollars bought from a bank in Caracas.*

An American sale of antibiotics will also appear on current account, because it creates income in the United States. But it will appear as a *credit* because it decreases the supply of goods available to Americans. It is listed next to *commodity exports* in Table 5. The transfer of dollars to pay for the drugs will show up in the cash account as a change in *foreign holdings of dollars*. It will be a *debit* there because it decreases American monetary liabilities to the outside world (Venezuelan holdings of dollars). In this case, the Venezuelan importer will buy a $300,000 draft from a bank in Caracas, paying with Venezuelan currency. He will send the dollar draft to the U.S. manufacturer who will deposit it in his own bank. Eventually, the draft will arrive at the New York bank at which the Venezuelan bank keeps its dollar balance, and it will deduct $300,000 from the Venezuelan's dollar account.

3. *The leasing of an American merchant ship for $50,000 by an Argentine exporter to carry frozen beef to Liverpool.*

This transaction is similar to an export sale; the American shipper contracts to provide a service using U.S. resources. Hence, the rental fee will appear as a *credit* on current account. If, next, the Argentine meatpacker pays $50,000 worth of Argentine currency (pesos) to rent the ship and the U.S. shipper sells them to his bank, there will be an increase in American holdings of Argentine currency, and this will appear as a *debit* (an increase of American cash claims on foreigners) in the cash account of Table 5.

4. *The building of a $400,000 factory in Italy by an American company, to assemble tractors for sale in the European Common Market.*

This transaction also appears in the U.S. balance of payments, although no goods or services cross our own frontiers. It represents the acquisition of an earning asset and will appear as a *debit* on capital account. It is called *direct investment* because it is an outright extension of American enterprise rather than a purchase of securities issued by a foreign firm. The costs of building the factory will be reflected in the cash account as a *credit* entry, appearing as a decline in U.S. holdings of Italian currency if the necessary lire are bought from an American bank having an account in Italy.

TABLE 5

A Hypothetical Balance-of-Payments Table
for the United States (Thousands of dollars)

Item		Credit (+)	Debit (—)
1. Current Account			
Commodity exports	(antibiotics)	300	
	(machine tools)	200	
Commodity imports	(tin)		280
Services	(shipping)	50	
Balance on current account		270	
2. Capital Account			
Direct investment	(factory)		400
Government lending	(India)		200
Balance on capital account			600
Balance on current and capital accounts			330
3. Cash Account			
Increase (+) in foreign holdings of dollars			
	(antibiotics)		300
	(factory)	400	
	(Indian loan)	200	
	(machine tools)		200
Net increase		100	
Increase (—) in U.S. holdings of foreign currencies	(tin)	280	
	(shipping)		50
Net decrease		230	
Balance on cash account		330	

5. *A $200,000 loan from the U.S. Export-Import Bank to the Indian government for the purchase of American-made machine tools.*

Since the Export-Import Bank is an agency of the United States government, the $200,000 loan will appear as a government transaction on capital account. It will be a *debit* because it generates a claim on India. It will also give rise to a *credit* on cash account—an increase in Indian holdings of dollar balances. When, however, the Indian government draws down its dollar balance to buy machinery, a *credit* entry will appear on current account; an export of machine tools will increase American income but reduce the supply of goods available to Americans. At the same time, a *debit* entry will appear on cash account.

Now total up the entries in each section of Table 5—the current, capital, and cash accounts. Notice that the balance on current account *plus* the balance on capital account must offset the balance on cash account. The excess of American spending abroad, including purchases of long-term earning assets, must match the net change in the American cash position. The United States is $330,000 richer in goods and earning assets, but poorer in cash by a like amount; it owes $100,000 more to foreign banks and holds $230,000 less of foreign currency. I shall call this reduction in the U.S. cash position the *gross payments deficit.*[1] It measures the gap between gross payments *from* the United States and gross payments *to* the United States.

In Table 5 the United States has a gross deficit even though it also has a current-account surplus. A country in deficit, then, may be quite capable of earning its way in world markets. Such a country is merely using some of its cash or credit to acquire extra earning assets. This is precisely what the United States has done during recent years. It is not necessarily a "bad thing." If a country starts out with a strong cash position, it may do well to run a deficit in order to acquire more earning assets. A deficit becomes dangerous only when it cuts so deeply into cash that a country can no longer cope with unplanned deficits arising from cyclical and other temporary disturbances—or when the deficit continues despite every effort to staunch it, so that citizens and foreigners alike begin to doubt the government's ability to control the situation.

A balance-of-payments table is designed to measure gross deficits or surpluses with the outside world.[2] But it tells us very much more. First, the current account shows how foreign trade affects aggregate income at home and abroad. In my example, Americans have earned $550,000 by selling goods and services to other countries; foreigners have earned $280,000. Second, the cash account shows what has happened to the money supply at home and abroad. Foreign banks have acquired an additional $100,000 of dollar balances; these funds came from Americans. American banks have lost $230,000 worth of foreign currency; these funds were paid to foreigners. Thus, the dollar bank deposits of Americans have fallen by $100,000, while the foreign-currency bank deposits of foreigners have increased by the equivalent of $230,000. Finally, the cash account also shows what has happened to the cash balances (inventories of foreign currency) held by banks. American

---

[1] It is sometimes called the "basic" deficit, but I prefer the term used in the text.

[2] In actual practice, however, it is not drawn up like Table 5, transaction by transaction. Instead, the statisticians gather all the data they can on each type of flow (goods, services, direct investment, and long-term lending), then try to reconcile the balance on current and capital account with the separate banking data on cash changes. They cannot do this perfectly, as many items escape the statisticians' net. Each country's balance-of-payments table, therefore, has a term that Table 5 lacked—an allowance for "errors and omissions" to fill the gap between the recorded surplus or deficit and the net change in the cash position. You will look at the actual U.S. balance-of-payments table in Chapter 5 and will find some other differences between Table 5 and the real thing.

banks have run down their balances by the equivalent of $230,000; foreign banks have increased theirs by $100,000.

Alternative Monetary Systems

The banks' foreign-exchange holdings play a strategic role in the international payments system. Each transaction in Table 5 drew upon or added to those balances, as the banks stood by to supply foreign currencies and U.S. dollars when traders and investors needed them. But the banks cannot let their holdings of foreign currency fall very low because they must have currencies on hand to make future sales. Nor can they allow their balances to rise very high because they would then tie up their assets in their foreign-exchange business and, more importantly, could suffer losses if exchange rates changed. The banks must keep close control over their inventories. Thus, in Table 5, foreign banks might seek to sell off all or part of the $100,000 increase in their dollar balances, and U.S. banks might seek to rebuild their holdings of foreign currency by all or part of the $230,000 decrease.

Suppose, then, that foreign banks seek to sell $50,000 and that U.S. banks seek to buy $130,000 worth of foreign currency. The foreign banks will enter the New York foreign-exchange market offering $50,000 in exchange for an assortment of pounds, francs, marks, and other foreign currencies. The American banks will enter the same market offering $130,000 in exchange for a similar assortment. The foreign-exchange market in which they operate is nothing more than a network of telephone connections between major banks and brokers. But it is much like any other market, where changes in supply and demand lead to price fluctuations. Later in this chapter, we will analyze the foreign-exchange market using supply-and-demand curves.

If foreign and American commercial banks try to buy $180,000 worth of foreign currencies ($50,000 *plus* $130,000), there will be an *excess demand* for foreign currency (an *excess supply* of dollars) in the foreign-exchange market. Such a situation will touch off a chain of events that will eventually react on the current and the capital accounts in the balance of payments. They will decrease the American demand for foreign currency and increase the foreign demand for U.S. dollars. They will thereby reduce the gross payments deficit, restoring equilibrium in the foreign-exchange market by forestalling further changes in the banks' working balances. But the nature and the sequence of these happenings will depend on the organization of the international monetary system—on the extent to which exchange rates can fluctuate and on the way the money supply is connected to a country's gold and foreign-exchange holdings. To illustrate, I shall describe three monetary systems and show how they would operate if there were an excess demand for foreign currency:

1. A system of *flexible exchange rates,* under which the price of foreign currency is left to fluctuate when there are changes in supply and demand. Here, exchange-rate changes will ordinarily operate to eliminate excess demand. The price of foreign currency will rise, making foreign goods more expensive for Americans and making U.S. goods cheaper for foreigners. Americans will buy fewer foreign goods, and foreigners will buy more U.S. goods.

2. A *pure gold standard,* under which the price of foreign currency cannot change because each currency has a fixed gold value. If one currency is worth 20 grains and another is worth 10, the first can always be exchanged for 2 units of the second. With an excess demand for foreign currency, gold will flow away from the United States, reducing its supply of money and, therefore, its price level. It will enter other countries, raising their supplies of money and, therefore, their price levels. These price-level changes will work just like exchange-rate changes, making foreign goods more expensive for Americans and making U.S. goods cheaper for foreigners. A gold flow will also alter interest rates and attract short-term capital to the United States.

3. A system of *managed exchange rates,* under which exchange rates are stabilized by official intervention in the foreign-exchange market. Here, too, money stocks may change, altering prices and the balance of payments. But there may be no strict link between the domestic monetary situation and the foreign-exchange market. Hence, price levels will not necessarily change. Governments may then be compelled to alter the exchange rates by changing their foreign-exchange policies.

PAYMENTS ADJUSTMENT UNDER FLEXIBLE EXCHANGE RATES

If exchange rates were free to fluctuate, an excess demand for foreign currency would cause the dollar to *depreciate.* It would depress the price of the dollar in terms of foreign currency or, what is the same thing, would raise the dollar price of foreign currency. This change in the exchange rate could, in turn, alter the flow of trade. If the French franc were selling for $0.25 to start, a French car costing 6,000 francs would sell for $1,500. An excess demand for foreign currency that raised the dollar price of the French franc to $0.40 would raise the dollar price of the French car to $2,400. Americans would buy fewer French cars. Similarly, an American machine costing $10,000 would at first sell for 40,000 francs, but only 25,000 francs after the depreciation of the dollar. French industry would buy more American machines. A decrease of U.S. automobile imports, however, will be reflected in the U.S. demand for foreign currency and, therefore, in the supply of dollars on the foreign-exchange market. Likewise, an increase in U.S. machinery exports will be reflected in the French demand for U.S. dollars.

Take U.S. exports first. The vertical axis in the upper panel of Fig. 12 shows the price of a U.S. machine in French francs. The vertical axis in the

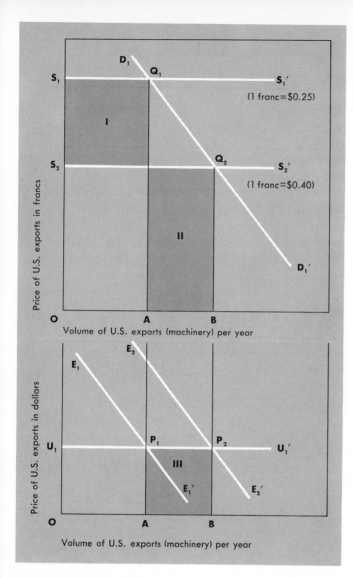

FIG. 12 Currency depreciation and the demand for exports. A depreciation of the dollar lowers the franc price of U.S. machines from OS_1 to OS_2. It can increase franc-spending on U.S. machinery (if rectangle I is smaller than rectangle II) or decrease franc-spending (if rectangle I is larger than rectangle II). But it must increase the French demand for U.S. dollars, as dollar-spending on U.S. machines will rise by $OU_1 \times AB$ (the area of rectangle III).

lower panel shows the price of the same machine in U.S. dollars. If, therefore, the domestic price of an American machine is OU_1 dollars and a dollar buys 4 French francs, the French franc price of the machine will be $4 \times OU_1$, or OS_1, above. The horizontal axis of both panels lists export volume calibrated in physical units (machines). It must be the same in both panels. The French demand for U. S. machinery is shown by the curve D_1D_1' in the upper panel, giving equilibrium at Q_1. The United States will export OA machines, receiving OAQ_1S_1 francs. Now, let the price of the dollar fall on the foreign-exchange market. The dollar price of an American machine need not change (U_1U_1' will not shift). But the franc price of American machinery must fall apace with the depreciation of the dollar. If the depreciation proceeds until the price of the franc rises from \$0.25 to \$0.40, the franc price of an American machine will drop to OS_3 and the supply curve facing French buyers will be S_2S_2' instead of S_1S_1'. Equilibrium will be displaced to Q_2, and French imports of American machinery will rise to OB.

The number of French francs spent on United States goods may either rise or fall with the depreciation. (It will fall if rectangle I is larger than rectangle II and rise if rectangle I is smaller than rectangle II.) But this ambiguity need not worry us. The increase in the volume of U.S. exports is all that is required to improve the balance of payments. This is because the dollar price of U.S. machinery has not changed, so that the French demand for dollars must rise when France buys more machinery. This fact is reflected in the lower panel of Fig. 12. There, the increase in the French demand for American machinery appears as a rightward shift in the demand curve (from E_1E_1' to E_2E_2'); from the standpoint of the American exporter, the French demand for machinery has increased at an unchanged dollar price. The French demand for dollars has consequently increased by $OU_1 \times AB$, the area of rectangle III.

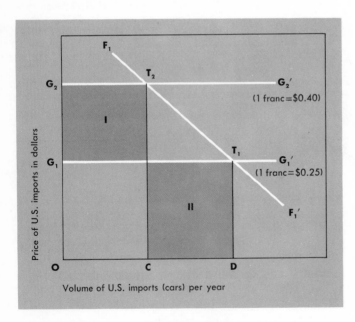

FIG. 13 Currency depreciation and the demand for imports. A depreciation of the dollar could raise or lower the supply of dollars on the foreign-exchange market. It will raise the supply if rectangle I is larger than rectangle II. It will lower the supply if rectangle I is smaller than rectangle II.

Consider, next, the impact of the depreciation on the supply of dollars. The vertical axis of Fig. 13 measures the dollar price of French cars and the horizontal axis measures the number of cars imported by the United States. If, to start, the supply curve is G_1G_1' and the demand schedule is

F_1F_1', there will be an equilibrium at T_1. Americans will import OD cars. If, next, the dollar depreciates by 60 per cent (the price of the French franc rises from \$0.25 to \$0.40), the dollar price of a French car will rise by 60 per cent, from OG_1 to OG_2. Equilibrium will be displaced to T_2 and the volume of imports will decline to OC.

What will happen to the supply of dollars on the foreign-exchange market? Notice that the change in United States spending on French cars can be divided into two parts. Rectangle I in Fig. 13 shows the first part—the extra dollar outlay per car bought after the depreciation. Rectangle II shows the second part—the decline in dollar outlay due to lower volume. If rectangle I were larger than rectangle II, a depreciation of the dollar would increase the supply of dollars. If rectangle II were larger than rectangle I, the depreciation would reduce the supply of dollars.[3]

But even if the supply of dollars grows when the dollar depreciates, there may still be a decline in the *excess supply* of dollars. The increase in demand can be larger than the increase in supply.[4] To see how depreciation

[3] In the economists' professional jargon, rectangle I will be larger and the supply curve of dollars will be positively sloped if the American demand for imports is *price-elastic;* it will be negatively sloped if the American demand for imports is *price-inelastic.*

[4] In professional jargon, depreciation will help to remove an excess supply of dollars if the sum of the *price-elasticities* of demand and supply is positive (if the supply curve cuts the demand curve from below).

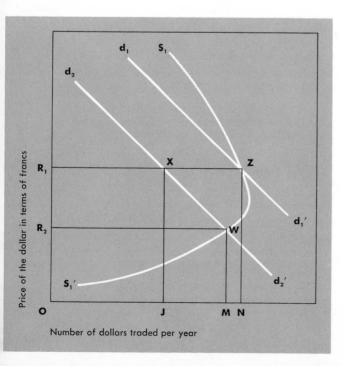

FIG. 14 Supply and demand in the foreign-exchange market. A decrease in the demand for dollars (a shift in the demand curve from d_1d_1' to d_2d_2') would cause the dollar to depreciate by R_1R_2. The dollar would buy fewer French francs and fewer francs would be needed to buy a dollar.

affects excess supply, look at Fig. 14. There, the vertical axis measures the price of the dollar in French francs, and the horizontal axis measures the number of dollars traded per year. The curve d_1d_1' is a demand curve for dollars, derived from the French demand curve for U.S. exports. It shows what you have already discovered—that the demand for dollars will increase as the price of the dollar falls. The curve s_1s_1' is a supply curve of dollars, derived from the U.S. demand curve for imports. It shows that the supply of dollars may move either way—that the amount supplied can actually decrease if the price of the dollar rises sufficiently. In a free market for foreign exchange, the exchange rate would settle at OR_1 francs to the dollar, for supply and demand are equal at that price. If, however, the foreign demand for U.S. goods fell, the foreign demand for dollars would also fall, shifting to d_2d_2'. At the old exchange rate, OR_1, there would be an excess supply of dollars, ZX or NJ, in the foreign-exchange market. The dollar would depreciate by R_1R_2, raising the number of dollars demanded by JM and lowering the number of dollars supplied by MN. The excess supply of dollars would disappear.

PAYMENTS ADJUSTMENT UNDER A PURE GOLD STANDARD

The old-fashioned gold standard furnished a simple system of fixed exchange rates and a way to regulate the quantity of money. Under the gold standard, each government defined its monetary unit (the dollar, pound, franc, etc.) in grains or ounces of gold metal, then stood ready to exchange gold for its currency and its currency for gold. Some governments went further, issuing gold coins, but this was not vital. The gold-standard mechanism worked as well where governments issued paper money fully backed by gold. Any change in central-bank gold holdings forced an equal change in currency outstanding (or in bank reserves).

There are vestiges of this arrangement in the American monetary system. The United States Treasury still buys gold from foreign governments at $35 per Troy ounce (less a small commission) and sells it at $35 an ounce (plus a small commission). The dollar, then, has a fixed valuation equal to 1/35 of an ounce of gold. Furthermore, the Federal Reserve Banks must hold $25 in gold certificates for every $100 of liabilities (Federal Reserve Notes outstanding and deposit obligations to the commercial banks). These certificates give them title to Treasury gold. But the United States does not sell gold to individuals, here or abroad. Nor is there any direct link between the U.S. gold stock and the supply of money in the United States. The Federal Reserve Banks can increase their liabilities (currency and bank reserves) without taking on more gold. They can buy government securities.

If all currencies were pegged to gold, and all governments were willing to trade currency for gold with private citizens as well as other governments, an *implicit* exchange rate would be established between each pair of currencies. If, for example, the French franc were freely exchangeable for gold at 140 francs per Troy ounce of gold, it would exchange for $0.25 in American currency; 140 francs would buy an ounce of gold and an ounce of gold would buy $35. Hence, 140 francs = $35, and 1 franc = $35/140 = $0.25. The actual exchange rates could still fluctuate a little bit, since governments might charge small commissions and bankers would have to pay the costs of shipping gold from one country to another. But when an exchange rate ran outside the boundaries set by these commissions and transport costs, the so-called "gold points," someone could profit by engaging in *arbitrage*. He could buy gold with the currency that was at a discount in the foreign-exchange market, sell it for the currency that was at a premium, and then exchange the second currency for the first. Suppose that the dollar slipped from $0.25 to $0.28 against the French franc and that it cost $0.10 in commissions and freight to ship an ounce of gold from New York to Paris. An *arbitrageur* could buy a thousand ounces of gold from the U.S. Treasury and ship them to Paris at a total cost of $35,100. He could sell the gold to the Bank of France for 140,000 francs, and then buy back dollars with the francs. As $0.28 × 140,000 = $39,200, he would make a $4,100 profit on his capital, or nearly 12 per cent, in a matter of days. He would also help to raise the price of the dollar, by exchanging francs for dollars at the end of his three-part transaction. Arbitrage would therefore serve to keep the exchange rates inside the "gold points" and quite close to the ratio of gold parities.

How would these transactions show up in a supply-and-demand picture of the foreign-exchange market (Fig. 14) and in the balance-of-payments statistics (Table 5)? With flexible exchange rates, a shift in the demand for dollars was met by a change in the price of the dollar; when the demand curve in Fig. 14 dropped from d_1d_1' to d_2d_2', the exchange rate changed from OR_1 to OR_2. With a pure gold standard, a shift in the demand curve would produce a gold flow, and this flow would keep the exchange rate stable. A drop in the demand curve in Fig. 14 would cause an outflow of gold from the United States, equal to XZ dollars per year. This gold loss would replace the excess supply of dollars in the foreign-exchange market. It would also show up as a *credit* item in the cash account of the balance of payments. The upper panel of Table 6 reproduces the cash account of Table 5. It shows the $100,000 increase in foreign holdings of dollars and the $230,000 decrease in American holdings of foreign currency. The lower panel of Table 6 shows the same account after foreign and American commercial banks have adjusted their balances. The foreign banks have sold $50,000; the American banks have acquired $130,000 worth of foreign currencies. The $180,000 worth of foreign currencies needed to finance these changes is supplied to the foreign-exchange market by gold arbitrage. The third step in arbitrage (the exchange of francs for dollars) supplies $180,000 worth of francs to the foreign-exchange market and takes $180,000 of U.S. currency out of the market. The last line of Table 6 records this gold arbitrage, showing a transfer of $180,000 worth of gold from the U.S. Treasury to the Bank of France.

Table 6 also supplies a new way to measure the U.S. deficit—by the change in official holdings of cash assets (gold and foreign currencies). I shall call this measure the *net payments deficit* and will use it from here on as the best measure of payments disequilibrium. It is better than the *gross deficit* concept because it corresponds to the notion of excess supply in the foreign-exchange market. Although there was a $330,000 gross deficit in Table 5, there was no pressure on the price of the dollar in the foreign-exchange market until commercial banks tried to adjust their inventories of foreign currency.

TABLE 6

Gold-Market Arbitrage and the Cash Account
in the U. S. Balance of Payments (Thousands of dollars)

A. The Cash Account before Gold-Market Arbitrage

	Credit	Debit
Privately held assets:	330	
Increase (+) in foreign holdings of dollars	100	
Increase (—) in U. S. holdings of foreign currency	230	

B. The Cash Account after Gold-Market Arbitrage

	Credit	Debit
Privately held assets:	150	
Increase (+) in foreign holdings of dollars	100	50
Increase (—) in U. S. holdings of foreign currency	230	130
Officially held assets:	180	
Increase (—) in U. S. gold stock	180	

It was this adjustment that gave rise to excess supply in the foreign-exchange market and caused the dollar to depreciate. It was this same change that caused gold-market arbitrage. And it will be this same change that brings official intervention in the foreign-exchange market under a system of managed exchange rates.

The notion of *net deficit* has another virtue. It identifies the cash flows that set off the most important monetary changes in the deficit and surplus countries. Under a pure gold standard, the country with a *net deficit* will suffer a decline in its money supply, while the country with a *net surplus* will experience an increase. These monetary changes are the direct results of the gold movements that measure the net deficit and surplus. They are unavoidable under a gold standard, as the central banks cannot offset them by open-market operations; the central banks can only hold gold. The pure gold standard guarantees to restore payments equilibrium.

To trace the process of adjustment under the gold standard, look at Table 7. The adjustment begins when a gold broker buys gold from the U.S. Treasury. The Treasury pays out $180,000 worth of gold in return for the broker's check. It deposits the check at the Federal Reserve Bank of New York, enlarging its balance there by $180,000 and replacing one asset (gold) with another (a bank deposit). The Federal Reserve Bank sends the broker's check to the commercial bank on which it was drawn, and deducts $180,000 from that bank's deposit balance, reducing one deposit liability to offset the increase in another. The commercial bank has lost $180,000 of its balance at the Federal Reserve Bank, but it can also balance its books. It deducts $180,-000 from the broker's own account when the broker's check arrives, reducing its liabilities to offset the decline in its assets.[5]

TABLE 7

Gold Flows and the U. S. Money Supply: Treasury, Federal Reserve and Commercial-Bank Balance Sheets (Thousands of dollars)

Institution and Item	Asset	Liability
U. S. Treasury		
Gold stock	—180	....
Balance at Federal Reserve Bank	+180	....
Federal Reserve Bank of New York		
Treasury deposit balance	....	+180
Member-bank deposit balance	....	—180
Commercial Bank		
Member-bank deposit balance	—180	....
Broker's deposit balance	....	—180

When these transactions have been completed, everyone will have balanced his books. But the process of monetary contraction is far from finished. If the commercial banks were "loaned up" (if they had no excess reserves) before the gold loss, they must now cut down their lending and deposits. Suppose that they must maintain a 10 per cent reserve ratio against their deposit liabilities. They will have to reduce their deposit obligations by a full $1,800,000, because they have lost $180,000 in reserve balances at the Federal Reserve. To do so, they must cut back their loans or investments by $1,620,000. This process is summarized in Table 8. When it is completed, the $180,000 gold loss will have caused the U.S. money supply to drop by $1,800,000.

[5] The chain of transactions may not end at this point. The Treasury may use its extra cash balance to retire $180,000 of gold certificates held by the Federal Reserve Bank. It may have to do so because it no longer has the gold that "backed" those gold certificates. But this additional transaction occurs within the government; it does not affect the commercial banks or the U.S. money supply.

TABLE 8

Gold Flows and the U. S. Money Supply:
Memorandum on Commercial-Bank Reserves (Thousands of dollars)

Initial decrease in deposit liabilities		180
Decrease in total reserves (member-bank balances)	180	
Decrease in required reserves (10 per cent reserve requirement against deposit liabilities)	18	
Reserve deficiency	162	
Secondary decrease in lending and deposits (due to deficiency)		1,620
Total decrease in deposit liabilities		1,800

These transactions are repeated in France, but run the other way. When the gold-market broker sells gold to the Bank of France, he receives a check drawn on the Bank of France. He will sell that check to move back into dollars, but the foreign-exchange dealer who buys the check from him will deposit it with a French commercial bank. That bank, in turn, will send the check to the Bank of France and receive an extra reserve balance. The French commercial banks will be empowered to expand their lending and the French money supply.

These vast monetary changes will change interest rates in the United States and France, affecting the current and capital accounts. A decrease in the U.S. money supply will raise U.S. interest rates; an increase in the French money supply will reduce French interest rates. Short-term capital will flow to the United States in search of higher yields, augmenting the demand for dollars in the foreign-exchange market. Domestic spending will decline in the United States and will rise in France, causing wage and price changes that work just like exchange-rate changes.

Interest rates and capital movements. An increase in U.S. interest rates relative to foreign rates can generate several types of short-term lending and investment. First, it may alter the pattern of borrowing and financing of foreign trade. An American importer who usually borrows dollars from a New York bank and converts them to sterling to pay for British goods may, instead, borrow sterling directly from a London bank. A British importer who ordinarily borrows dollars in New York to pay for American goods may, instead, borrow sterling in London, then swap it for dollars to pay for his purchases. American importers who borrow in London reduce the supply of dollars in the foreign-exchange market. British importers who borrow in London increase the demand for dollars. Changes in the *locus* of borrowing will therefore reduce the excess supply of dollars. Next, a change in interest rates can foster explicit cash transfers. A British corporation that normally invests its idle funds in London by buying British Treasury bills will send its money to New York to buy U.S. Treasury bills or other money-market instruments. An American corporation that normally holds money in London to finance its foreign operations may transfer cash to New York to earn a higher interest rate. These two transfers will also increase the demand for dollars.

But these short-term capital flows can only aid the dollar temporarily. Money that is borrowed today must be repaid in a few months. Furthermore, there is a built-in market mechanism working to arrest the transfer of funds. When American importers borrow in London and British firms place cash in New York, they face the risk that the dollar will depreciate. If this were to happen, the American importer would have to spend more dollars to repay his sterling debt, and the British company would get fewer pounds for the dollars it had placed in New York.[6] To protect themselves against this exchange risk, investors and borrowers can arrange *forward foreign-exchange contracts*. They can promise to deliver dollars for pounds at some future date but at an exchange rate fixed in the contract. The *forward foreign-exchange rates* fixed in the contract, however, may be quite different from the *spot rates* at which currencies are traded for immediate delivery. Investors may therefore incur extra cost. Furthermore, the forward dollar-sterling rate will tend to move in sympathy with the interest differential and offset the incentive to move funds to New York. When interest rates are higher in New York than in London, the pound sterling tends toward a premium on the forward exchange market (see Fig. 15). This is because importers borrowing in London and companies investing in New York both buy forward sterling to *hedge* against exchange risks and thereby increase the demand for forward sterling. But as they bid up its price, they raise the cost of hedging and cancel the interest-rate differential.

To sum up, an interest-rate differential caused by changes in the stock of money can help to remove a payments deficit. But it cannot do the whole job. A more lasting change is needed to remove an excess supply of dollars. The pure gold standard has also to change costs and prices.

Interest rates, spending, and prices. Early economic theory connected the supply of money and domestic prices by a simple axiom: If the supply of money falls, prices have to fall, so that the remaining currency can do its work efficiently. The early writers on international finance consequently argued that a gold standard would be self-adjusting. A gold transfer from Britain to France would reduce British prices and raise French prices; the citizens of both countries would buy more British goods and fewer French goods; Britain

---

[6] This risk is much greater with managed exchange rates than with a pure gold standard. But it existed even in the heyday of the old gold standard, before 1914. The exchange rates could still move within the "gold points" and the gold parities could be changed.

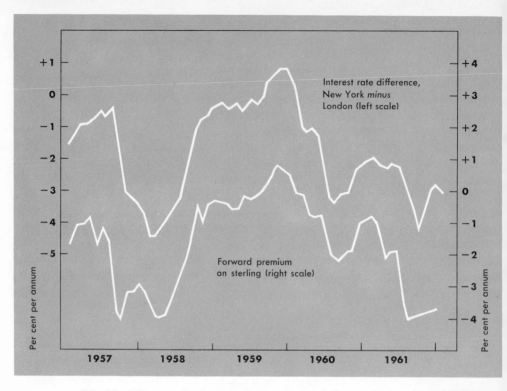

FIG. 15 Differences in short-term interest rates and the premium on forward foreign exchange. When New York interest rates are above London interest rates, the pound rises to a premium in the forward foreign-exchange market. When London interest rates are above New York interest rates, the pound falls to a discount. The relationship is even closer than the lines indicate; the right scale has been lowered to disentangle the two lines. (Source: International Monetary Fund, *International Financial Statistics*, various issues.)

would develop a surplus on current account; gold would start to flow back to Britain. David Hume, the eighteenth-century philosopher, put this *specie-flow theory* very neatly:

> Suppose four-fifths of all the money in Great Britain to be annihilated in one night, and the nation reduced to the same condition, with regard to specie, as in the reigns of the Harrys and Edwards, what would be the consequence? Must not the price of all labour and commodities sink in proportion, and everything be sold as cheap as they were in those ages? What nation could then dispute with us in any foreign market, or pretend to navigate or to sell manufactures at the same price, which to us would afford sufficient profit? In how little time, therefore, must this bring back the money which we had lost, and raise us to the level of all the neighboring nations? Where, after we have arrived, we immediately lose the advantage of the cheapness of labour and commodities; and the farther flowing in of money is stopped by our fulness and repletion.

But even if wages and prices moved smoothly, the connection between prices and the money stock would be less direct than Hume implied. Most economists would first link the supply of money to the rate of interest, then link the interest rate to total spending, spending to employment, and employment to wage rates. Then they would come to prices.

A drop in the quantity of money is apt to increase interest rates because it is accomplished by a cut in bank lending. It involves a decline in the supply of loanable funds, and a cut in supply will raise the price of credit—the rate of interest. When interest rates increase, however, aggregate spending will fall. Some forms of business investment are quite sensitive to interest rates or to the credit rationing that may accompany any rise in interest rates. A reduction in investment, moreover, reduces every form of private spending; a *multiplier* process is set to work reducing consumption along with investment. Finally, a reduction in aggregate spending will lead to a reduction in output and employment, and a decline in employment will cause workers to bid down money wage rates, cutting costs and prices.

From here on, the argument is much like Hume's own exposition, but with one qualification. Lower prices in the country losing gold and higher prices in the country gaining gold will increase the exports of the deficit country and reduce its imports. This will improve its balance of payments and stem its gold loss, provided the changes in volume are larger than the changes in price. But just as one would normally expect exchange depreciation to improve the balance of payments, so one would expect deflation to do the same thing. The gold-standard mechanism and exchange-rate changes have similar effects if wage rates are flexible. The chief difference is that an exchange-rate change moves one crucial price, whereas the gold standard keeps that price constant and moves all the rest.

PAYMENTS ADJUSTMENT UNDER MANAGED EXCHANGE RATES

Although the United States pegs its currency to gold, we do not have a pure gold standard. The Federal Reserve Banks can hold other assets (government securities) against their monetary liabilities (Federal Reserve Notes and member-bank deposits), so that there is no strict link between gold-stock changes and the American money supply. Furthermore, other governments do not peg their currencies to gold, so that there is no implicit exchange rate between the dollar and other currencies. Yet most countries still keep their exchange rates stable. Instead of holding gold as "backing" for their currencies and passively awaiting gold-market arbitrage, they have established exchange stabilization funds under central bank or treasury control. These funds hold mixed portfolios of foreign currencies and gold, and use these reserves to finance intervention in the foreign-exchange markets. When the price of a country's currency rises, its exchange stabilization fund sells domestic currency for foreign currency, reducing the price. It adds the foreign currency to its own reserves. When the price of a currency falls, the exchange stabilization fund buys domestic currency with foreign currency, raising the price. It takes the foreign currency out of its reserves. In Fig. 14, for example, the Bank of France might buy up ZX dollars, the excess supply, to keep the exchange rate stable at OR_1. It would put French francs into the foreign-exchange market and take out dollars. The Bank of France could retain these dollars or convert them into gold at the U.S. Treasury.[7] The Bank of France need not act as soon as the exchange rate begins to change. Under the rules of the International Monetary Fund, however, it must intervene whenever the exchange rate moves by as much as 1 per cent from its announced parity. This 1 per cent margin is akin to the range allowed by the "gold points."

If the Bank of France decides to buy gold with the dollars it takes from the foreign-exchange market, the U.S. cash account will look just as it did under the gold standard (Table 6). If it holds onto the dollars, the numbers in the cash account will be the same as they were in Table 6, but the last line will read "Increase $(+)$ in foreign official holdings of dollars."

If the Bank of France buys gold with its dollars, the American money supply will begin to fall, as it did in Tables 7 and 8. If it decides to hold the dollars, there will still be a decline in the money supply, but the process will differ from that of the gold standard. Many central banks keep their dollars on deposit with the Federal Reserve Banks. If the Bank of France decides to do so, it will draw a check on the New York commercial bank where its dollars lay when it first acquired them from a French foreign-exchange dealer. It will send the check to the Federal Reserve Bank of New York, which will credit the Bank of France with $180,000 and deduct the same amount from the account of the New York commercial bank. The commercial bank's reserves will fall by $180,000, and it will be compelled to reduce its loans or investments. There will also be an increase in the French money supply. The Bank of France will create new French francs when it buys dollars from the foreign-exchange market, and these francs will find their way into the reserves of the French commercial banks.

If this were all that could happen with managed exchange rates, the system would work like a pure gold standard. There would be an increase in U.S. interest rates and a drop in French rates. Short-term capital would flow toward the United States. Prices would begin to change here and abroad, altering the current account and stemming the deficit. But something else can

---

[7] Thus the size of U.S. gold flows relative to U.S. payments deficits depends on the reserve-asset preferences of foreign governments and central banks. If the United States runs a payments deficit *vis-a-vis* countries whose central banks usually hold the dollars they acquire, the U. S. payments deficit need not lead to a gold loss. If it runs a deficit *vis-a-vis* countries whose central banks normally hold gold, like Britain, France, and Switzerland, it will almost always lose gold as a result of its deficit. The United States can also lose gold when it does not have a payments deficit. This may happen when a dollar-holding country runs a deficit with a gold-holding country, transferring dollar deposits to a central bank that will use them to buy gold. It can also lose gold when a foreign central bank alters its reserve-asset portfolio.

happen with managed exchange rates. The Federal Reserve Banks may not allow the money stock to decline. They may buy government securities in the open market to replenish American bank reserves and forestall a contraction in lending and deposits. The Bank of France may sell government securities to reduce French bank reserves and forestall an increase in lending and deposits.[8]

Central banks are quite apt to follow these policies—to "neutralize" gold and foreign-balance changes. Look at Table 9 to see two episodes in which the Federal Reserve Banks offset heavy gold flows. In 1939–1941, the U.S. gold stock rose by $5.2 billion. Part of this increase was allowed to

TABLE 9

**U.S. Gold Stock and Commercial-Bank Reserve Balances
at the Federal Reserve Banks (Millions of dollars)**

Item	1939-1941	1959-1961
Change in U.S. gold stock	+5,241	—2,554
Change in foreign deposits at the Federal Reserve Banks	+ 792*	— 132
Net foreign influence (gold *less* deposits)	+4,449	—2,422
Federal Reserve credit, currency in circulation, and Treasury operations	—3,108	+1,050
Total (equals change in commercial-bank reserve balances at the Federal Reserve Banks)	+1,341	—1,372

* Includes the change in "other" domestic deposits which cannot be separated from foreign accounts for these years.
Source: Board of Governors of the Federal Reserve System, *Federal Reserve Bulletin.*

increase bank reserves, but most of it was offset by domestic operations. In 1959–1961, the U.S. gold stock fell by $2.5 billion. Part of this decline was allowed to reduce bank reserves, but much of it was also offset by domestic operations.[9]

Domestic and External Equilibrium

Why should central banks offset external disturbances when, by doing so, they interfere with the processes that can restore payments equilib-

[8] Both central banks can also change the reserve requirements under which their commercial banks operate. The Federal Reserve System can reduce the U.S. reserve ratio. The Bank of France can raise the French reserve ratio. They can thereby align the reserve requirements with the actual change in reserves.

[9] On this occasion, moreover, there was no decrease in bank lending or deposits, as the banks had just been allowed to count their vault cash toward reserve requirements, and this change in the rules more than offset the decline in member-bank balances by adding $2.5 billion of vault cash to reserves.

rium? Why did the Federal Reserve Banks neutralize so large a part of the U.S. gold loss in 1959–1961, allowing the United States to go on running deficits?

The answer is quite simple. To achieve payments equilibrium by domestic deflation is much more painful than I have allowed you to suppose. Wage rates and prices do not fall easily or quickly. A decline in domestic spending brought about by an increase in interest rates (or by fiscal policy) will lead to unemployment, not to wage reductions. If the United States sought to reach external balance by following the gold-standard rules, it would have to sacrifice full employment. Its imports would still shrink as domestic spending fell. But the decline in imports would be caused by a reduction in real income, not by a reduction in prices. Furthermore, a payments deficit can sometimes depress income and employment directly, and governments are loathe to compound this direct effect. They may even try to combat it.

NATIONAL INCOME AND FOREIGN TRADE

To understand the links between exports, imports, and the level of employment when costs are rigid, you must start with the basic income identities.[10] In an open economy (one with foreign trade), three types of spending contribute to the national income:

C Consumption (household spending)
I Investment (business spending)
X Exports (foreign spending

But each of these three streams includes spending on imported goods as well as domestic products. Therefore, deduct imports, M, from total spending to define domestic income, Y:

$$Y = C + I + X - M$$

This arithmetic relationship tells half the story. Three of the four spending streams listed in the basic income equation are also affected by income itself.

Consumption, exports, and imports depend quite directly on national income. Given an extra dollar of income, consumers will usually spend a fraction of a dollar more on goods and services. This connection is a basic building block of economic analysis. Imports and exports depend on prices and exchange rates, but also respond to changes in income. Imports will increase with income at home. Exports will increase with income abroad (being the imports of some other country). If, indeed, prices and exchange rates are stable, the income-import connection will be much like the link between

---

[10] This analysis ignores the role of government expenditure, as its inclusion would complicate the analysis without changing the result.

income and consumption. A dollar more of income will give rise to a fractional increase in the demand for imports.[11]

The remaining component of income, business investment, depends on many things, and income may be one of them. But we will suppose that investment is governed by the rate of interest—that it will rise when the interest rate falls, and will fall when the interest rate rises. On this assumption, monetary policy will affect national income by affecting investment.

The two-way relationship between trade and income gives rise to an important balancing mechanism. Suppose that there is a change in foreign tastes that causes a decline in exports. This decline will produce a payments deficit, but will also cut back national income. The reduction in income will then reduce import spending, narrowing the payments deficit. And income will actually fall more than exports because the decline in income will include a decline in consumption. Hence, the reduction in imports may be quite large.

But the induced decrease in imports may not be great enough to match the entire drop in exports; there may still be a payments deficit when national income and imports have ceased to change. As consumers tend to save part of an increase in income and cushion any drop in income by saving somewhat less, the decrease in income is apt to cease before it has cut imports by as much as exports fell. You can see how this happens by working through the numerical example in Table 10. Savings and imports each fall by 50 in the first stage; the drop in savings is the difference between the drop in income (250) and the drop in consumption (200). Taken together, then, savings and imports combined have changed by as much as exports. But because savings have fallen, imports have not dropped enough to restore payments equilibrium.

In order to re-establish payments equilibrium, the government must foster a further drop in the national income and thereby depress spending on imports. It must let the payments deficit cut into the supply of money and may even have to hasten this contraction by open-market operations; it must end

---

[11] Actually, the income-import link may be a percentage relationship, rather than a fractional (linear) relationship; in the professional jargon, the *marginal propensity to import* may not be constant, but the *income-elasticity of demand for imports* may be nearly constant. As evidence, look at these figures bearing on imports and gross national product during two recent cyclical upturns in the United States:

	Percentage Change	
	Imports	G.N.P.
First quarter 1958 to second quarter 1959	+22.9	+12.7
First quarter 1961 to second quarter 1962	+19.7	+10.2

The ratio of the change in imports to the change in G.N.P. (the *income-elasticity of demand for imports*) works out at 1.8 in the first upturn and 1.9 in the second upturn. These figures, however, may be a shade higher than the long-run income-elasticity of demand because they refer to cyclical income swings and include a large amount of inventory investment in imported products.

TABLE 10

Changes in Income and Its Components Due to a Decline in Exports
(The marginal propensity to consume is 0.8; the marginal propensity
to import is 0.2.)

Period	Income from Last Period (1)	Consump- tion (2)	Invest- ment (3)	Exports (4)	Imports (5)	Current Income (6)	Trade Balance (7)
First Stage: An autonomous decrease in exports							
1	0	0	0	—100.0	0	—100.0	—100.0
2	—100.0	— 80.0	0	—100.0	— 20.0	—160.0	— 80.0
3	—160.0	—128.0	0	—100.0	— 32.0	—196.0	— 68.0
4	—196.0	—156.8	0	—100.0	— 39.2	—217.6	— 60.8
...	...	...	...	...	...	...	...
...	...	...	...	...	...	...	...
Final	—250.0	—200.0	0	—100.0	— 50.0	—250.0	— 50.0
Second Stage: A decrease in investment induced by higher interest rates							
1	—250.0	—200.0	—100.0	—100.0	— 50.0	—350.0	— 50.0
2	—350.0	—280.0	—100.0	—100.0	— 70.0	—410.0	— 30.0
3	—410.0	—328.0	—100.0	—100.0	— 82.0	—446.0	— 18.0
4	—446.0	—366.8	—100.0	—100.0	— 89.2	—477.6	— 10.8
...	...	...	...	...	...	...	...
...	...	...	...	...	...	...	...
Final	—500.0	—400.0	—100.0	—100.0	—100.0	—500.0	0

Explanation of Entries
　(1) Income of the previous period carried over from column 6.
　(2) Four-fifths of the entry in column 1.
　(3) An independent variable; there is no change in investment during the first stage, then a 100
　　　drop in the second stage due to an increase in interest rates.
　(4) An independent variable; there is a 100 drop in the first stage.
　(5) One-fifth of the entry in column 1.
　(6) The sum of current consumption, investment and exports less imports (2 + 3 + 4 — 5).
　(7) Current exports *less* current imports (4 — 5).

the deficit before it has eaten up the country's reserves of gold and foreign currency. A drop in the supply of money will raise interest rates and depress domestic investment. A cut in investment spending will reduce the national income. This process is shown in the second stage of Table 10.

But payments equilibrium can only be restored at an enormous cost. There have been two doses of deflation in this example (the initial cut in exports and the later cut in domestic investment). Each one has been magnified by the multiplier. Furthermore, the reduction in imports will reduce some other country's income. A deflation in one country is apt to spread to others through foreign trade.

To sum up, rigid costs make deflation a painful way to maintain external balance. Governments are always tempted to offset the monetary shrinkage that would otherwise occur automatically. There may be a sharp conflict between policy objectives—the need to maintain payments equilibrium and to foster full employment. One such conflict arose in the 1930's when many countries were afflicted with mass unemployment. It was, indeed, to escape this conflict that so many countries imposed tariffs, quotas, and exchange controls—the sad story I recounted in Chapter 3. The problem, moreover, is still with us. Several countries, including the United States, have felt constrained to tolerate high unemployment rates in order to combat prolonged payments deficits.

ADJUSTMENT AMIDST ECONOMIC GROWTH

The process of adjustment under fixed exchange rates would not be so painful if wage rates were flexible. It may not be so painful if adjustment is imbedded in global economic growth. A country in deficit can then change its costs even though its wage rates are rigid. It can also work to alter national expenditure without creating massive unemployment. It can tamper with the rates of increase in wages and expenditure, not with the absolute levels.

Suppose, first, that labor productivity is rising steadily in all countries. If a deficit country can hold its wage rates constant, while foreign wages rise apace with productivity, costs and prices will decline in the deficit country, and its balance of payments is apt to improve without any absolute loss of output or employment.

Suppose, next, that output and money incomes are growing together in all countries, so that prices do not change. If the deficit country can keep its domestic expenditure from rising apace with output, it will be able to hold down its imports and to enlarge its capacity to serve foreign markets. It will experience a gradual improvement in its balance of payments.

But these growth-rate effects are more easily described than achieved. Although they have a cumulative impact, moreover, they work very slowly. Payments deficits and surpluses may endure for quite a while, straining international financial arrangements. The maintenance of payments equilibrium is among the most painful tasks governments must face.

Summary

Foreign economic policy has two major dimensions. An open economy must formulate *commercial* policies to reap the gains from foreign trade and foreign investment. It must formulate *financial* policies to maintain monetary equilibrium in its foreign transactions.

The choice of an exchange-rate regime is the first step in making international financial policy. With exchange rates free to fluctuate as market forces dictate, a difference between foreign payments and receipts will show up as excess supply or excess demand in the foreign-exchange market. An excess supply of the domestic currency will cause its price to decline (depreciate); an excess demand will cause it to increase (appreciate). A change in the exchange rate will alter the foreign price of a country's exports and the domestic price of its imports. It will have the same effect as a change in the country's over-all price level. If foreign currency becomes more expensive, there will be an increase in the foreign and domestic demand for home goods (a shift away from foreign goods), which will restore equilibrium in the foreign-exchange market.

With exchange rates fixed by the gold standard or official intervention in the foreign-exchange markets, an excess supply of home currency will bring about a contraction in the domestic money supply and an expansion in the foreign money supply. These monetary changes will also work to restore equilibrium, though differently from flexible exchange rates. They will raise interest rates in the deficit country and depress them in the surplus country. The change in interest rates will call forth money flows and cause price changes that adjust the current account.

With rigid costs and prices, however, the bulk of the adjustment must take place through income changes. Some of these changes occur directly and automatically. A decrease in exports will reduce national income, cutting domestic expenditure on home goods and imports. Some of the changes are indirect, brought on by monetary policy. Higher interest rates in the deficit country will depress investment, reducing national income and compressing imports. These indirect effects will continue to operate until the deficit is ended. The money supply will go on shrinking, interest rates will go on rising, and investment will continue to fall, reducing income and imports. With fixed exchange rates and rigid wage rates, however, governments may face an intractable policy conflict. They may have to choose between full employment and payments equilibrium.

5

INTERNATIONAL FINANCIAL POLICY

The Choice Among Exchange-Rate Regimes

The world's monetary system was most like the gold standard during the 40 years before the First World War. By the mid-1870's, each major country had connected its currency to gold, establishing a fixed exchange rate between its own currency and all the others. After the completion of the Atlantic Cable, linking London and New York, the market exchange rates stayed quite close to their gold parities, and the parities did not change until 1914.

Governments did not give up all control over the supply of money. They did not base their currencies wholly on gold. In the United States, for example, banks could issue paper money backed by their holdings of government securities. In Britain, the Bank of England bought and sold commercial bills and government securities to ease or tighten credit. But Britain and some other countries usually adhered to the "rules of the game"; they used monetary policy to reinforce rather than offset the impact of gold flows.

Yet the international payments system did not work quite as theory said it should. The major countries sometimes corrected their payments positions by altering output and employment rather than prices. They sometimes shifted the burden of adjustment onto countries at the periphery of the monetary system—the raw materials producers of the Western Hemisphere and other outlying areas. A tightening of credit in Britain bore heavily on the financing of trade in raw materials because this trade was financed with money lent by London. When British interest rates were high and credit scarce in London, dealers had to compress their inventories, cutting the prices of raw materials and reducing Britain's import bill. The countries at the periphery, moreover, changed their exchange rates rather often, dropping away from the gold standard during payments crises, then returning at different gold parities.

After the First World War had wrecked the monetary system, the statesmen tried to build a new gold standard. This attempt ignored the differences between pre-war theory and pre-war practice. But it might even have failed if the builders had understood the pre-war system, for the environment had changed. First, there was less flexibility in the international economy; you have already read of the growth in inter-government debt, the increase in tariffs and the wide use of quotas, and the huge expansion in farm output. Second, there was less strength at the center of the international financial system; Britain's chief exports, textiles and coal, were meeting fierce competition in foreign markets, while New York and Paris had become major purveyors of capital and credit, so that London could no longer influence world money markets as before the war. Third, there was less tolerance of unemployment; new political parties drawing support from urban workers threatened any government that dared to use deflation to cure its payments problems. Governments, moreover, had found new ways to insulate the national economy from international monetary changes. New central banks had been established in several countries, including the Federal Reserve System in the United States, and all the central banks had found new ways to contravene the "rules of the game." Finally, the structure of international reserves had changed. Many countries were holding dollars and pounds sterling, as well as gold coin and gold bullion. Sterling was the more important of the new reserve-assets; some countries held the bulk of their reserves as sterling balances invested in

London. Even the Bank of France, a pillar of monetary orthodoxy, built up large sterling claims in the 1920's. The new system, then, was a *gold-exchange standard,* not a simple gold standard.

This last change in the monetary system was inspired by widespread fears of a future gold shortage and was sanctioned by international financial conferences. But it proved to be a major weakness. Britain had become the banker to other governments and was continually threatened by a run on its own small gold reserves—just like any other banker with no central bank to serve him as lender of last resort. The run finally came in 1931, and dealt the new system its death blow. In 1925 Britain had pegged the pound at its old gold parity, taking no account of the increase in British prices or the weakness of Britain's export industries. As a result, the United States and France ran large payments surpluses. The United States masked its surplus by heavy long-term lending to other countries—by huge private purchases of newly issued foreign bonds. France took in gold and built up its sterling claims. With the collapse of the American economy in 1929–1930, American lending came to a halt. In 1928 there was a net capital outflow (—) of $1,541 million; in 1931, there was a net inflow (+) of $756 million:

	Millions of Dollars	
	1928	1931
Direct investment (—)	— 558	—222
Purchases of new foreign bonds (—)	—1019	—190
Redemptions of foreign bonds (+)	361	257
Other long-term capital (net)	— 94	283
All short-term capital (net)	— 231	628
Total	—1541	756

In 1931, new purchases of foreign securities were not even large enough to cover redemptions, let alone the massive repatriation of other capital. At about the same time, moreover, the French legislature instructed the Bank of France to convert its sterling holdings into gold, putting heavy pressure on the pound. Britain was compelled to leave the gold standard in the summer of 1931, when a panic that had started with the collapse of the *Credit Anstalt,* the Rothschild bank in Vienna, spread across Europe and began to lap at Britain's gold reserves.

The 1930's saw complete monetary chaos. Many small countries had left the gold standard in 1929 and 1930. Many others followed in 1931 and 1932. Their currencies fluctuated in the foreign-exchange market, propelled by underlying economic changes and by waves of speculation. Then the United States devalued the dollar; it left the gold standard in 1933 and came back to gold at a lower parity in 1934. The countries that had stayed with gold, including France and Italy, imposed new trade barriers to protect their currencies and economies against competition from countries that had left the gold standard. Some governments went further, seeking to generate an export surplus and increase employment at the expense of other countries. The situation was not brought under close control until 1936, when France and other gold-bloc countries changed their gold parities and made a "stand-still" agreement with Britain and the United States, barring a new round of competitive depreciation. When the exchange rates had finally settled down, they were not much different from what they had been before 1931. Here are the percentage depreciations (—) in key currencies, based on 1930 exchange rates with the U.S. dollar:

	1932	1933	1934
United Kingdom	—33	+ 2	+ 1
India	—32	+ 2	+ 1
Australia	—41	—12	—13
Canada	—13	+ 1	0
Italy	0	+62	0
Belgium	0	+68	+21
France	0	+68	+19

The Commonwealth countries (India, Australia, and Canada) moved with Great Britain; their currencies depreciated through 1932 (as the pound left gold in 1931), but strengthened relative to the dollar by 1934 (as the dollar left gold in 1933). The gold-bloc countries, by contrast, showed no change until 1934, when they suffered an involuntary appreciation because of the drop in the gold price of the dollar. By 1936, however, much of this premium vanished because the gold-bloc countries changed their own gold parities.

Summing up the 1920's and 1930's, one observer drew these conclusions:

> The twenty years between the wars have furnished ample evidence concerning the question of fluctuating *versus* stable exchanges. A system of completely free and flexible exchange rates is conceivable and may have certain attractions in theory. . . . Yet nothing would be more at variance with the lessons of the past. . . . In the first place, they create an element of risk which tends to discourage international trade. . . . Secondly, as a means of adjusting the balance of payments, exchange fluctuations involve constant shifts of labour and other resources between production for the home market and production for export. . . . Thirdly, experience has shown that . . . any considerable or continuous movement of the exchange rate is liable to generate anticipations of a further movement in the same direction, thus giving rise to speculative capital transfers of a disequilibrating kind. . . .[1]

This view had an enormous impact on the monetary system which rose from the wreckage of the Second World War.

[1] Ragnar Nurkse, *International Currency Experience* (Geneva: League of Nations, 1944), pp. 210-211.

THE BRETTON WOODS SYSTEM

This time, the governments avoided one of the grave errors they had committed after the First World War. They tried to deal separately with the needs of post-war reconstruction, rather than burdening the international monetary system with a new layer of indebtedness and straining the new exchange rates with abnormal import needs. The U.S. Lend-Lease program gave outright aid to America's allies in order to forestall the accumulation of new inter-allied debts. The large U.S. loan to Britain in 1945 and the Marshall Plan in 1948 sought to finance reconstruction without drawing off the gold reserves of the war-shattered countries or saddling them with huge short-term debts.

The governments likewise sought to establish new exchange rates by general agreement and to keep them stable once they had been fixed. They did not eschew all exchange-rate changes, preferring devaluation [2] to exchange control, trade control or deflation. Devaluation is much better than exchange or trade control because it does not distort resource allocation. It increases the foreign demand for domestic goods at the same time it limits the domestic demand for foreign goods. Import controls, by contrast, increase the domestic price of import-competing products, attracting domestic resources away from the more efficient export industries. Devaluation is much better than deflation because it does not depress employment or impede economic growth. In modern economies with wage and price rigidity, deflation leads to unemployment before it lowers prices. And every major government is pledged to maintain maximum employment and to foster rapid economic growth.

The new exchange-rate system was enshrined in the Bretton Woods Agreement of 1944, which established the International Monetary Fund (IMF) and erected the framework for post-war monetary cooperation. Governments agreed to peg their currencies to gold or to the U.S. dollar (which is pegged to gold). They agreed to make their currencies convertible—to dismantle their exchange controls—after a transition period. And they agreed on rules for policing exchange-rate changes. A government may alter the par value of its currency by as much as 10 per cent without IMF approval, but needs the Fund's approval for a larger change. This approval, moreover, will only be forthcoming when a country faces a "fundamental disequilibrium" in its international accounts.

The Bretton Woods system, sometimes called the system of the *adjustable peg,* seeks to assure maximum exchange-rate stability, yet to facilitate orderly change when it is needed and to avoid competitive devaluations like

[2] I shall henceforth use the term *devaluation* when I mean a once-over change in a fixed exchange rate (accomplished by changing the gold parity or the price at which the central bank intervenes in the foreign-exchange market). I shall use the term *depreciation* when I mean a change in a flexible exchange rate (accomplished by trading in the open market).

those of the 1930's. There have been a number of important exchange-rate changes under the Bretton Woods system. In 1949, for example, Britain devalued the pound from $4.03 to $2.80, and was followed by many other countries in Europe and the Commonwealth. France devalued the franc in 1957, and Germany and the Netherlands raised their parities in 1961. Exchange-rate changes have been most frequent at the periphery of the international economy—especially in Latin America—just as they were in the nineteenth century. The less-developed countries have had difficulty maintaining price stability while promoting rapid growth; they lack the wide range of policy instruments available to countries with advanced money markets and fiscal systems, and have been afflicted by wide fluctuations in the prices of their major export products.

THE CASE FOR GREATER FLEXIBILITY

A growing group of economists, however, argues that the Bretton Woods regime combines the disadvantages of fully fixed exchange rates with the disadvantages of flexible exchange rates.

First, they say, the Bretton Woods system encourages countries to employ undesirable methods of payments adjustment. Because it treats an exchange-rate change as the remedy of last resort and because such a change becomes quite conspicuous rather than an every-day occurrence, governments hesitate to alter their exchange rates. They tend to regard devaluation as a confession of failure. Hence, some governments still resort to trade controls (or refuse to dismantle them), thus distorting resource allocation. Other governments keep a tight rein on domestic demand, using restrictive monetary and fiscal policies; they forego economic growth to maintain payments equilibrium. This has been a common criticism of British policy—and of recent American policy as well. More generally, critics say, the present regime imparts a deflationary bias to the whole process of payments adjustment. A country that runs a payments deficit will eventually use up its reserves. But a surplus country can accumulate reserves indefinitely.[3] A deficit country may therefore be obliged to deflate or devalue its currency, while a surplus country cannot be compelled to inflate or appreciate. With flexible exchange rates, on the other hand, the market operates with an even hand, raising the price of the surplus country's currency and lowering the price of the deficit country's currency.

Critics also accuse the present system of fostering perverse capital move-

[3] A surplus country may have difficulty offsetting the monetary impact of its payments surplus. To sop up the commercial-bank reserves created by a surplus, the central bank must engage in open-market sales of government securities or must raise commercial-bank reserve requirements. The central bank can run out of government securities. And by increasing reserve requirements, it ties up the assets of the commercial banks, diminishing the banks' rate of profit. These things were happening in Germany in 1958-1961, when Germany experienced a massive payments surplus, the counterpart of the U.S. deficit, discussed below.

ments that aggravate more basic payments problems. Speculation can be *destabilizing,* even as it was in the 1920's and 1930's, when exchange rates changed often. This is because traders and investors can "attack" a weak currency at negligible cost. Suppose that the price of the pound has fallen as far as it can with its present parity (from $2.80 per pound to $2.78) and that Britain's currency reserves are slipping away as the Bank of England uses them to support the exchange rate. Speculators know that Britain cannot lose reserves forever and may begin to gamble on the possibility that Britain will devalue the pound. Some will sell sterling securities they have been holding. Others will borrow in London rather than abroad, hoping to repay their debts with cheaper pounds. These flows and others will add to the pressure on the price of the pound and force the Bank of England to use still more reserves to support the existing exchange rate. If devaluation was a possibility before speculation began, it can become a near certainty once speculation is underway.

If Britain does devalue the pound, the speculators will make handsome profits; a 20 per cent devaluation will give them a 20 per cent gain (less the income they have foregone by using their financial resources in speculation). If the pound is not devalued, speculators can unwind their positions without much loss; they can buy the pounds they need at very little additional cost. At worst, the pound will rise to its upper limit, $2.82, forcing the speculators to pay a 4 cent premium on the pound when rebuilding their sterling holdings and paying off their sterling debts. But 4 cents on $2.80 is a mere 1.4 per cent—hardly a high price to pay for the chance of gaining 20 per cent from devaluation.

Speculators can also attack weak currencies under a system of flexible exchange rates. But speculation would be much more costly, for the price of the pound could rise without limit, compelling speculators to unwind their positions at a huge premium. Furthermore, some experts say, a system of flexible exchange rates would actually engender *stabilizing* speculation, rather than *destabilizing* speculation. Speculators would strengthen weak currencies.

The debate on this point has grown quite complex. But the basic point at issue is still very simple. The advocates of flexible exchange rates argue that a drop in the price of any asset will attract more buyers, not more sellers. As a currency weakens in the foreign-exchange market, speculators will come to regard it as a bargain and will start to buy it. Doing so, they will arrest the price decline, even cause the currency to appreciate. Likewise, as a currency appreciates, speculators will come to think that it is priced too high and will start to sell it. Doing so, they will arrest the price rise. If these propositions are true, speculation will dampen exchange-rate fluctuations, not amplify them.

This analysis of speculation builds on the implicit supposition that there is a trendless "normal" rate to guide the speculator when he makes his judgments about future exchange rates. If there were no "normal" rate (or if it had a trend), speculators could not be so certain that a falling rate would soon start to rise or that a rising rate would soon start to fall. They might consequently buy as rates began to rise and sell as rates began to fall. The importance of a "normal" rate showed up clearly in the 1950's, when the Canadian dollar was allowed to fluctuate: The exchange rate stayed within a rather narrow range; speculation may have been helpful. But the speculators were probably guided by a fixed norm. When the Canadian dollar rose above its old parity with the United States dollar, it dropped to a discount on the forward market. Speculators apparently thought the spot rate was "too high," basing their judgments on the old parity.[4]

This need for a "normal" rate implies that exchange-rate flexibility may in fact work best when the underlying disturbances do not call for wide fluctuations. If large exchange-rate changes are required and the rate drifts away from the familiar range, speculators may not know which way to turn and may operate in a destabilizing manner.

There is one more objection to flexibility. It could build an upward bias into world prices. Depreciation and devaluation raise the domestic prices of imported goods; this is how they discourage imports. In countries that import foodstuffs or industrial materials, however, an increase in import prices raises the cost of living and calls forth a demand for higher wages. A wage-rate increase, in its turn, raises prices further—including export prices. In brief, an exchange-rate change can touch off a wage-price spiral, offsetting the competitive advantage initially conferred by the depreciation or devaluation. If, of course, the wage-rate rise is quite small, a depreciation will still rectify a payments deficit, and a country faced with a deep-seated payments problem should accept a depreciation. But what of the country whose foreign payments display a cyclical pattern? During a recession its balance of payments is strong; during a boom its balance of payments is weak. If its exchange rate fluctuated freely, its currency would depreciate during the boom, adding to domestic inflationary pressures. It would, of course, appreciate again during the next recession. But its wage rates might not come down again. With flexible exchange rates, then, the domestic business cycle would raise wages and prices in a step-wise fashion.

One could adduce another dozen arguments on each side of this issue— and as many intermediate positions. Some economists, for example, think that fixed parities are needed, if only to provide speculators with some sort of "norm," but advocate wider exchange-rate variations than the Bretton Woods agreement allows. These wider variations, they contend, would raise the cost of speculating against weak currencies. If the pound could fall as low as $2.70 and rise as high as $2.90, speculators would lose 20 cents on the pound by

---

[4] G. Paul Wonnacott, *The Canadian Dollar, 1948-1958* (Toronto: University of Toronto Press, 1960), p. 138.

selling it at its low and buying it back at its high. And 20 cents on $2.80 is a 7 per cent loss, much larger than the present 1.4 per cent.

But the major governments do not favor more flexibility, not even wider margins around fixed parities. There is actually a trend in the opposite direction. The Canadian dollar was allowed to fluctuate for almost 12 years, then was pegged again in 1962. Many central banks oppose any change in the price of a key currency (the dollar, pound, franc, mark, or lira), for one change can touch off rumors of a second and a third, as with the 1961 appreciation of the deutschemark. They would apparently rely on the gradual processes of economic growth to make needed changes in national expenditure and relative prices, and would ride out deficits and surpluses by committing their reserves in support of the existing exchange rates.

The New Gold-Exchange Standard

The major central banks seem to have enough reserves to cope with speculation in the foreign-exchange market and to buy the time needed for these gradual adjustments. By the end of 1962, central banks and governments held some $61.3 billion of gold and foreign currencies (Table 11), a sum fully half as large as the dollar value of world exports and more than 10

TABLE 11

International Monetary Reserves, 1951 and 1962
(Billions of dollars; end of year)

Country	1951	1962
United States	$22.9	$16.1
United Kingdom	2.4	2.8
Total, reserve centers	25.3	18.9
European Economic Community *	3.5	16.9
Canada and Japan †	2.8	4.3
Other developed countries ‡	4.2	7.2
Total, all developed countries	35.8	47.3
Other European countries	1.8	3.0
Latin America	3.0	2.3
Other Asian and African countries	8.5	8.7
Total, less-developed countries	13.2	14.0
Total, all countries	49.0	61.3

* Belgium-Luxembourg, France, Germany, Italy, and the Netherlands.
† First figure for Japan is for 1952.
‡ Austria, Denmark, Norway, Sweden (1952), Switzerland, Australia, New Zealand, and South Africa.
Source: International Monetary Fund, *International Financial Statistics* (August, 1963).

times the largest annual reserve flow (the sum of all recorded deficits) in the late 1950's. The bulk of these reserves, moreover, was held at the center of the international monetary system. A full $35.8 billion belonged to eight governments—the United States, United Kingdom, and six countries of the European Common Market. Reserves were more markedly concentrated than a decade before. The developed countries, taken as a group, increased their reserves by $11.5 billion between 1951 and 1962, and the EEC countries increased their reserves almost fivefold.

Most authorities are consequently satisfied with the present level of reserves, even though the distribution could be improved. Continental Europe may have more reserves than it needs; Britain does not have enough, given the importance of sterling as an international currency; and the less-developed countries have far too few cash assets. Latin America has actually lost reserves since 1951.[5]

But many experts are worried about the composition of reserves and about future expansion. Outside the United States, reserves are evenly divided between gold and currency (Table 12). The U.S. dollar is the leading reserve currency, accounting for a quarter of other countries' assets. But the United States has actually supplied more than 75 per cent of the increase in reserves since 1951. It has supplied $7.9 billion of dollar assets and $6.7 billion of gold (the other $5.5 billion of gold coming from new production and Soviet sales). The $6.7 billion U.S. gold loss and $7.9 billion increase in

[5] If, of course, one *gave* reserves to the less-developed countries, they would spend them in their efforts to develop, rather than hold them for emergencies. When, therefore, I say that reserves could be better distributed, I do not mean that they *should be* redistributed—only that the less-developed countries do not hold enough cash (by choice or otherwise) to cope with emergencies.

TABLE 12

The Composition of International Monetary Reserves, 1951 and 1961 (Billions of dollars; end of year)

Country and Asset	1951	1962
United States	22.9	16.1
Gold	22.9	16.0
Foreign exchange	0	0.1
All Other Countries	26.2	45.2
Gold	11.0	23.2
Foreign exchange	15.1	22.0
of which: U. S. dollars	4.0	11.9
Sterling *	8.7	6.6
All other †	2.4	3.5

* Includes Commonwealth securities.

† The 1962 entry may include some dollars held outside the United States and some official holdings of long-term dollar securities.

Source: International Monetary Fund, *International Financial Statistics* (various issues).

TABLE 13

The International Investment Position of the United States, 1951 and 1962
(Billions of dollars; end of year)

Item	1951	1962
American Assets		
1. Official monetary assets (gold, convertible currencies, and subscriptions to the IMF)	25.6	20.3
2. Private monetary assets (claims on foreigners)	1.7	7.2
3. Private direct investments abroad	13.0	37.1
4. Other private long-term investments abroad	6.2	15.4
5. Other government claims on foreigners	11.3	19.2
6. Total assets	57.8	99.2
American Liabilities		
7. Monetary liabilities to foreign governments and international institutions *	5.2	17.3
8. Monetary liabilities to other foreigners †	4.5	9.5
9. Foreign holdings of long-term U.S. government securities	1.5	2.1
10. Foreign private direct investments	3.4	7.6
11. Other foreign long-term investments	4.6	12.6
12. Total liabilities	19.2	49.1
Excess of Assets over Liabilities:		
13. All assets less all liabilities (6–12)	38.6	50.1
14. Official monetary assets less official monetary liabilities (1–7)	20.4	3.0

    * Figure for 1962 includes $5.1 billion of obligations to international institutions and $0.3 billion of special Treasury obligations to foreign governments; these account for the difference between this figure and the corresponding line in Table 12.
    † Includes U.S. currency held abroad.
Source: United States Department of Commerce, Survey of Current Business (August, 1962); Board of Governors of the Federal Reserve System, Federal Reserve Bulletin (July, 1962); and Banking and Monetary Statistics, Supplement 15 (March, 1962).

U.S. debts are the consequence of an 11-year net deficit in the American balance of payments.

The United States is quite far from insolvency, despite this deterioration in its own reserve position. Table 13 shows that the total foreign assets of the United States far exceed its total liabilities, and that the excess of assets over liabilities (line 13) has grown tremendously since 1951. But some foreign observers are not impressed by this calculation. They look at the U.S. *cash* position, and this has weakened markedly since 1951. There has been a $17.4 billion decline in U.S. monetary assets compared to U.S. monetary debts (line 14 in Table 13).[6]

A few years ago, no one would have talked of a run on the dollar, but such talk is heard too often today. In fact, there was a short-lived run on the dollar late in 1960, when private investors and a handful of governments cashed in dollar assets to buy gold, and drove the free-market price of gold

    [6] This figure does not match the cumulative gold loss and increase in debts mentioned earlier because it includes changes in other official assets and in debts to international institutions.

from $35 to $42 an ounce. This sort of behavior is silly. The United States government still has $20 billion of monetary assets, including almost 40 per cent of the world's gold stock. Its reserves are sufficient to cope with many more years of deficit and it does not have to contemplate devaluation or exchange controls.

Yet the connection between the U.S. balance of payments and the U.S. balance sheet as an international banker may still be unhealthy for the United States and for the international monetary system. An ordinary bank can expect its assets and liabilities to move in the same direction. When its customers draw down their deposits, the bank's cash holdings and obligations fall together. But the United States may lose cash assets when its liabilities increase and gain cash when they fall. Its balance sheet as an international banker is connected to its transactions as a producer, consumer, and investor—to its balance of payments. When the United States slips into deficit, it loses gold and incurs adlitional debt. When it moves into surplus, it gains gold and pays off debt.

Suppose, as an analogy, that an ordinary commercial bank were owned and operated by an automobile company that merged its own balance sheet with that of its bank. If the auto company suffered losses, it would draw on the cash assets of its bank. The bank would lose cash (but not pay off deposits) when its parent company had a bad year and would gain cash (but not gain deposits) when its parent company had a good year. The American balance of payments affects the U.S. balance sheet in much the way the auto company's profit-and-loss statement would affect the balance sheet of its banking affiliate. When the United States runs a payments surplus, its "bank" gains cash and pays off depositors. When it runs a deficit, its "bank" loses cash and incurs additional deposit liabilities.

Under the fictitious arrangements I have just described, a bank owned by a stricken auto company might someday succumb to a run. This is why our laws forbid such an arrangement. The United States faces an analogous danger. Its depositors may switch to gold when it runs a long or large deficit in its international transactions.

Gold and foreign-exchange holdings play a strategic role in the international payments system. They are the buffers that shelter the system from unwanted instability. Government and academic experts have therefore been seeking ways to strengthen the international monetary system:

1. Ways to cope with shifts in the reserve-asset preferences of the central banks—with shifts from dollars into other currencies or from currencies to gold.

2. Ways to redistribute reserves between the advanced and less-developed countries and to provide for a further increase in total reserves when it is again required.

These two problems are closely connected. To solve the first, for example, the United States must control its balance of payments. This would bolster foreign confidence in the dollar as a reserve currency and reduce the likelihood of a shift away from the dollar. But then the second problem might grow more acute. The U.S. deficit has been the chief source of reserves for other countries, and new gold production plus Soviet gold sales might be too small to furnish sufficient reserves for the future. To solve the second problem, governments might increase the price of gold, as this would raise the dollar value of existing gold stocks and new gold production. But an increase in the price of gold would damage confidence in the dollar and, therefore, aggravate the problem of stability.

THE ROLE OF THE INTERNATIONAL MONETARY FUND

Most proposals for reform of the international monetary system look to a strengthening or reconstruction of the International Monetary Fund. The IMF cannot create reserves, but it does make them "go around" more efficiently. It is a pool of currencies and gold furnished by its 76 member governments. When a country joins the IMF, it is assigned a *quota* which governs the size of its cash subscription, its voting power, and its drawing rights. The United States has the largest quota ($4,125 million), Panama the smallest ($0.5 million). A member country pays a quarter of its quota in gold and the balance in its own currency. Thus, the United States has paid in $1,031 million of gold and $3,094 million of special U.S. government securities.

When a country encounters a payments deficit and does not have sufficient reserves to cope with the problem, it can buy foreign currency from the IMF in exchange for its own currency, but it must repurchase its own currency within 5 years. A member of the IMF can always buy foreign currency equal in value to a quarter of its quota (the equivalent of its initial gold subscription). To make a larger purchase, it must satisfy the Fund that it is trying to solve its payments problem, as by controlling domestic inflation. Thus, the Fund is able to exert substantial influence on national financial policies.

The IMF can often mobilize money from governmental lending agencies and private credit institutions. In 1958, for instance, it sold $75 million of U.S. dollars to Argentina. At the same time, the American government provided $200 million in loans through the Export-Import Bank, the Development Loan Fund, and the Treasury's Exchange Stabilization Fund; and American commercial banks supplied another $54 million in short-term credits. The IMF was consequently able to mobilize $329 million in credits to Argentina by committing $75 million of its own resources and approving Argentina's stabilization program. As the Fund's former Managing Director put it:

. . . when a country is clearly in such an unbalanced position that radical measures are required to restore equilibrium, private banks may properly be deterred by the risks involved in granting it further credit facilities. In such situations, it is only if a comprehensive program is adopted and put into effect that the risks will be reduced; and private institutions are not in a position to negotiate such programs. Experience has shown that the Governments in the various countries are more willing to discuss and work out stabilization programs with officials of the Fund than with representatives of other countries or of private credit institutions.

The IMF has proved its usefulness. In its first 16 years, it supplied 12 different currencies to 43 countries. Britain has been the largest single beneficiary of IMF assistance, as Britain's own reserves are quite small. Foreign observers have forecast a devaluation of the pound whenever Britain has run a payments deficit, and the British government has often had to cope with a massive short-term capital outflow. The less-developed countries have also used IMF resources. They, too, have small reserves and chronic payments problems. Their imports have risen rapidly because of their efforts to stimulate development. And most of them earn their way in world trade by exporting raw materials—coffee, tin, copper, or petroleum—products that are subject to wide price fluctuations.

Because of its great success and the respect it enjoys, many experts would expand the IMF to improve the world's monetary system.

First, they advocate a periodic increase in IMF quotas and a liberalization of the rules that regulate drawing rights. An increase in quotas, they maintain, could substitute for a straightforward increase in national reserves. Admittedly, a government would have to put more gold into the IMF to obtain a higher quota. But it will obtain a 4-dollar increase in its quota (and a larger increase in its borrowing power) for every dollar's worth of gold it pays in.

Second, they advocate special credits to protect the key currencies against speculation and to forestall shifts in the composition of reserves. Although the Fund's total assets exceed $15 billion, its *usable* assets are much smaller. At June 30, 1963, its holdings of the major currencies looked like this:

Gold	$3.2 billion
United States dollars	3.0 "
Sterling	1.4 "
EEC currencies	1.1 "
Other key currencies	1.2 "
Total	$9.9 "

And the Fund cannot use all these assets at the same time. If the United States dollar were in trouble, the Fund could not use dollars to help out; it would have to use gold and other convertible currencies. Some reformers have therefore proposed that the IMF be authorized to borrow key currencies directly from governments—francs from France, marks from Germany, and so on. It could then re-lend them to countries afflicted with deficits or speculative capital movements.

This two-part proposal has found great favor in official circles. In fact, the Fund has already moved far along these lines. In 1959 there was a general increase in IMF quotas. In 1962 the United States and key European governments agreed on a procedure for lending their currencies to the IMF if it should need additional assets to finance a major drawing. This agreement is not automatic, nor sufficiently flexible; each government retains the right to decide how much it will lend—if anything at all. But most governments would probably honor their promises if the Fund needed extra cash.

The IMF has already shown how it can help to combat speculation against a key currency. It did so directly during the Suez crisis of 1956, when it supplied $561 million to Great Britain and promptly frightened off the speculators. It did so indirectly in 1961 when it *refinanced* a series of special bilateral credit arrangements (the Basle agreements) between Britain and other European countries. The appreciation of the deutschemark and the Dutch guilder had touched off rumors that the pound would soon be devalued. Britain consequently suffered a large outflow of short-term capital and was in danger of exhausting its reserves. The European central banks came to Britain's aid by buying pounds in the foreign-exchange market and lending their own currencies to the British government. Britain's debts under these bilateral arrangements reached $900 milllon—an impressive measure of intergovernmental cooperation. Then, in the summer of 1961, the British government bought $1,500 million of foreign currencies from the IMF and used some of this money to repay the European central banks. In effect, the Fund consolidated Britain's bilateral indebtedness.

But some experts, while welcoming a stronger IMF, are still dissatisfied. They would like to sever the connection between the U.S. balance of payments and the international monetary standard because an American payments deficit can still undermine the monetary system. Furthermore, the United States cannot change its own exchange rate without disturbing the connection between gold and the dollar, the two most important reserve assets. Finally, these critics say, an increase in IMF quotas may not be a satisfactory substitute for larger national reserves. They still urge a major reform of international monetary arrangements.

The leading advocate of thorough reform is Professor Robert Triffin of Yale. He has suggested that the International Monetary Fund be transformed into a central bankers' bank—that central banks be obliged to place a percentage of their gross reserves on deposit with the IMF, and that these deposits be denominated in a new international unit of account.[7]

This arrangement, Triffin says, would have two advantages. First, deposits at the IMF would carry a gold guarantee. If there were an increase in the dollar price of gold (a devaluation of the dollar), an IMF deposit would not be affected, whereas a dollar deposit would buy less gold after the devaluation. Governments would have little cause to change the composition of their reserves. Second, the IMF could enlarge total reserves in much the same way that an ordinary central bank enlarges the reserves of its commercial banks. It could create a new type of money. Instead of selling foreign currency to a country needing more reserves, the Fund would make straightforward loans, creating new deposits to the credit of the borrower. The borrower could then draw on its IMF deposit to settle its deficits with other governments—or could use its balance to buy foreign currencies for use in the foreign-exchange markets. Finally, the International Monetary Fund would be authorized to buy national securities in the open market, much in the manner of a central bank, in order to create more IMF money and thereby enlarge world reserves.

Triffin's plan would limit lending by an expanded IMF. It could be no larger than required to augment reserves by, say, 3 or 4 per cent a year. The plan would allow a central bank to convert its "excess" Fund deposits into gold or currency—to dispose of Fund deposits it was not obliged to hold under the prevailing reserve ratio. Thus, no country would have to accept indefinite amounts of IMF deposit money and thereby finance another country's deficit.

Other plans have been devised to repair defects in Triffin's proposal. Still others would connect the creation of new IMF deposits to the international financing of economic development. Under these plans, the IMF would buy bonds from the less-developed countries, supplying them with extra capital. Alternatively, the Fund could buy IOU's from intergovernmental agencies like the International Bank for Reconstruction and Development, supplying these agencies with IMF deposits. They would then lend these deposits to the less-developed countries.

But all these plans have met with frowns from central banks and finance ministries. There is an understandable resistance to radical reform—which goes deeper than doubt about technicalities. A prominent American official has summarized the major objections:

[7] Triffin has proposed that they be required to deposit 20 per cent of their gross reserves with the IMF, but believes that most governments would voluntarily keep a larger fraction on deposit with the Fund, as IMF deposits would earn interest and be guaranteed against exchange-rate changes. Triffin's plan, incidentally, has distinguished ancestors, including a similar proposal by Lord Keynes, who urged it as a rival to the United States plan for the IMF when the Fund was set up in 1944.

The money created by a super-bank would be the most high-powered ever generated by a man-made institution, yet it would have no supporting super-government to make good on its debts or claims. Even with all the underlying resources of the richest nation on earth, the performance of the United States in providing additional reserves has been at times rather conspicuously called into question. And in our case, the world has the basic assurance that our performance will continue broadly to meet the tests of economic requirements because otherwise pressures can be exerted upon us through our own balance of payments. There will be no comparable assurance, and no comparable underlying strength in the new body.[8]

The United States Payments Problem

The piecemeal innovations of 1959–1961 have one thing in common with the Triffin plan and its cousins: All of them require that the United States cut down its payments deficit or end it altogether. No amount of financing, no special arrangements, can sustain world confidence in the dollar if the American gold stock gets smaller and smaller, while American monetary liabilities get larger and larger. In consequence, the payments deficit has become a chief target of U.S. policy.

The United States has run payments deficits since the early 1950's. In 1958, however, the deficit grew very large and refused to close again. A part of this increase may be blamed on the inflation of the 1950's. Table 14 shows that U.S. export prices rose more rapidly than those of most other countries. The over-all (consumer) price index was more stable here than abroad, but the increase in U.S. steel prices raised many export prices. This country did not lose much ground in world markets despite the more rapid rise in its export prices. Nor did it gain enough ground to cover its increasing payments for goods and services or its larger foreign investments.

The United States customarily exports much more than it imports. But then it spends large sums for military purposes, lends large sums to the less-developed nations, and invests large sums in plant and equipment to serve foreign markets. The data for 1961, summarized in Table 15, will help to show what has happened during recent years.[9] The United States sold some $4.3 billion more of goods than it bought from foreigners. It earned $3.3 billion more in interest and dividends on its foreign investments. But then it

---

[8] Robert V. Roosa, "Assuring the Free World's Liquidity," *Business Review Supplement,* Federal Reserve Bank of Philadelphia (September, 1962), p. 8. Mr. Roosa is Under Secretary of the Treasury for Monetary Affairs.

[9] This table shows just one of many ways in which the data are sometimes arranged. I have tried to construct it to resemble the hypothetical balance-of-payments table in Chapter 4. To do so, I have put all short-term capital movements into the cash account, even though some of these transactions are commercial lending and belong in the capital account. I have also put the errors-and-omissions item in the cash account, on the (tenuous) supposition that most of the unrecorded transactions represent short-term capital transfers that escape the statisticians' net.

spent more for services than it received, and laid out large sums to maintain its military forces abroad. In the end, therefore, the current-account surplus was $4 billion smaller than the trade surplus—too small to finance the $6.2 billion outflow on long-term capital account. Hence, the gross deficit was a full $2.1 billion. Foreign governments made advance repayments on their post-war debts and provided other special aid in order to reduce the United States deficit; the deficit to be financed by reserves and short-term capital was only $700 million. But the *net* deficit, at $2.2 billion, was inflated by an outflow of U.S. private short-term funds. In fact, the private cash account has enlarged the net deficit in each of the last 3 years, rather than absorbing part of the strain on U.S. reserves. This capital outflow was not chiefly due to doubts about the future of the dollar, as in 1960. Some of it represented lending to other countries that had payments problems of their own.

What, then, can be done about the American deficit? Some people have urged that the United States lop off its large payments to the outside world—especially its foreign aid. At first glance, after all, this seems to be a troublemaker. But the problem is not quite this simple. If the United States cut its foreign aid, its exports would also decline, reducing the current-account surplus. Fully $3.2 billion of total government grants and loans were spent in the United States.[10] What is more important, foreign aid and military spending are vital parts of a larger policy shaped to foster the security and

[10] The government has already moved to "tie" its grants and loans to the purchase of American products. It cannot do so, however, with all its aid dollars. Nor can it prevent foreigners from using "tied" aid to buy American goods they would have bought anyway, then using "earned" dollars to buy goods from other industrial countries.

TABLE 14

**Percentage Increase in Prices, 1953 to 1962,
Major Industrial Countries**

Country	Consumer Prices	Export Prices *
United States	+13	+10
Belgium	+12	— 5
Canada	+14	— 1
France	+52	— 7
Germany	+20	+ 7
Italy	+27	—15
Japan	+31	— 8
Netherlands	+29	+ 3
Sweden	+34	+ 3
Switzerland	+16	....
United Kingdom	+31	+12

* Corrected for changes in exchange rates relative to the U. S. dollar
Source: International Monetary Fund, *International Financial Statistics* (August, 1963).

TABLE 15

The U. S. Balance of Payments in 1962 (Millions of dollars)

Item	Credit (+)	Debit (—)	Balance
1. Current Account			
Merchandist exports (+) and imports (—)	20,479	16,145	+4,334
Ordinary service transactions			
Transport, travel and tourism	2,670	3,960	—1,290
Income on investments	4,322	995	+3,327
All other (including private transfers)	1,659	1,572	+ 87
Military transactions	660	3,028	—2,368
Balance on current account			+4,090
2. Capital Account (except short-term funds)			
Government grants and loans (—) and loan repayments (+)	617	4,036	—3,419
Increase (—) in other government claims, net			— 245
Private direct investment, Americans (—) and foreign (+)	132	1,557	—1,425
Other private investment, American (—) and foreign (+)	139	1,209	—1,070
Balance on capital account			—6,159
Gross or "basic" deficit			—2,069
Special government receipts *			+1,280
Gross or "basic" deficit after deducting special government receipts			— 789
3. Cash Account			
Privately held assets			—1,448
Increase (+) in foreigners' dollar holdings †	84		
Increase (—) in Americans' claims on foreigners †		507	
Errors and omissions, net		1,025	
Officially held assets (net deficit)			+2,237
Increase (+) in foreigners' dollar holdings ‡	704		
Increase (—) in the U.S. reserves §	1,533		

* Includes advance repayments of government debt by foreigners, prepayments against U.S. military exports, and long-term U.S. Government securities transferred to international financial institutions as part of the U.S. capital subscription.

† Includes commercial credit.

‡ Includes special Treasury obligations issued to foreign governments.

§ Gold, convertible currencies, and IMF position.

Source: United States Department of Commerce, *Survey of Current Business* (June, 1963).

prosperity of the non-communist world. From the standpoint of the balance of payments, they must be taken as things given, and other items must be adjusted to make room for them.

To make the problem still more difficult, the United States must refrain from changing its exchange rate or imposing exchange controls. Either of these policies would damage the gold-exchange standard. It must instead influence its capital account by monetary policy and by promoting rapid economic growth to attract more foreign and domestic investors. The United States must also strive to increase its exports. It must encourage

American industry to maintain its technological leadership; it must raise its productivity by fostering investment in new plant and equipment; it must keep factor prices—wage rates and profits—from eating up its gains in productivity. These policies will exploit the growth effects discussed in Chapter 4. They will take time to take hold, but the United States still has the time it needs if it uses its time well.

Summary

Well before the end of the Second World War, governments began to plan for the reconstruction of the international monetary system. Determined to avoid another round of violent exchange-rate changes like the ones that followed the First World War, they decided to fix the new exchange rates at the very start of the post-war period and to foster orderly change thereafter. In the Bretton Woods agreement of 1944, establishing the International Monetary Fund, they agreed to forego devaluation unless the balance of payments had slipped into "fundamental disequilibrium."

One can make a strong case against the present system. By pegging exchange rates, it pegs the one set of prices that could change with sufficient ease and speed to maintain payments equilibrium. And by compromising between perfect fixity and full flexibility, it invites destabilizing capital movements that add to payments deficits. Finally, one can argue that a free market would choose the "right" exchange rate more often than a finance minister or central banker.

Yet there are grave objections to full flexibility, and some of the defects of the present system could be removed if the gold-exchange standard were strengthened or reformed—if exchange rates were allowed to vary more widely around their fixed parities and if the supply of reserves could be disconnected from the American balance of payments.

You have met several plans fashioned to attain these aims—plans to increase quotas in the IMF and lend the Fund additional cash; and plans that would transform the IMF into an international central bank that could create reserves on its own initiative.

Finally, you have glanced at the U.S. payments problem and examined the constraints on American policy that make it so difficult for the United States to end its deficit. The United States must take the slow road to equilibrium—eschewing cuts in foreign aid or controls on trade and capital movements.

6

TOWARD AN INTERNATIONAL ECONOMY

The Center and Periphery

At the start of Chapter 2, I suggested that a country's economic history has a great effect on its comparative advantage. Its stocks of capital and skill may influence its foreign trade more than its store of raw materials, climate, or terrain. These stocks are the legacies of economic history—of investments made in years gone by. These investments, in turn, were influenced by earlier trade patterns, reflecting existing market opportunities. The evolution of the international economy has been a cumulative process. Export opportunities, affecting the volume and pattern of investment, shaped countries' stocks of capital equipment. These stocks of equipment and the skills that go with them gave rise to new production possibilities, creating new trade patterns.

The role of trade in economic development has been especially significant for new countries—including the United States. The resource endowments of these countries—their stocks of capital and skill—were shaped by contact with the older countries of the international economy. As John Henry Williams of Harvard put it:

> . . . the development of international trade has been a process in which the countries outside the centre have owed the development of their trade, and indeed their very existence, to the movement, not merely of goods but of capital, labour, and entrepreneurship from the centre; and the centre countries have in turn owed their further development primarily to this movement. Western Europe created the modern world and was in turn remade by it. Any theory of international trade that does not approach the subject-matter in this way must have very serious limitations as a guide to policy.[1]

The late Ragnar Nurkse of Columbia dwelt on this same theme:

> . . . The industrial revolution happened to originate on a small island with a limited range of natural resources, at a time when synthetic materials were yet unknown. In these circumstances economic expansion was transmitted to less-developed areas by a steep and steady increase in Britain's demand for primary commodities which those areas were well suited to produce. Local factors of production overseas, whose growth may in part have been induced by trade, were thus largely absorbed by the expansion of profitable primary production for export. On top of this, the center's increasing demand for raw materials and foodstuffs created incentives for capital and labor to move from the center to the outlying areas, accelerating the process of growth-transmission from the former to the latter.[2]

Some economists hold to the hope that trade can still serve as an "engine of growth" to quicken the development of Africa, Asia, and Latin America, and that private capital will venture out from the center of the world economy—from Europe and the United States—to find new raw materials and create new industries. But others are not optimistic. They believe that the center countries will have to make special efforts in aid of develop-

---

[1] John H. Williams, *Trade, Not Aid: A Program for World Stability*. The Stamp Memorial Lecture, 1952 (Cambridge: Harvard University Press, 1953), p. 10.

[2] Ragnar Nurkse, "Patterns of Trade and Development," reprinted in *Equilibrium and Growth in the World Economy* (Cambridge: Harvard University Press, 1961), p. 285.

ment. Otherwise, powerful disintegrative tendencies will widen the great gulf between the rich and poor countries.

First, they point out that the nineteenth century's new countries were quite different from today's less-developed countries. The United States, Canada, and Australia lay in the temperate zones and had vast quantities of land with very little labor. They could supply the grain and cotton Europe required. Furthermore, they were peopled by immigrants with European institutions and values. Most of today's less-developed countries lie in the tropics and are very heavily populated. What may be more important, they are not islands of European civilization, but have institutions and values of their own.

Second, trade patterns have changed since the nineteenth century. The center countries' need for raw materials is not growing quite so fast as in the nineteenth century. Production at the center tends to be resource-saving rather than resource-using; the raw-materials content of final output is a smaller fraction of the whole than a century ago because value added by processing is so much larger. Furthermore, the development of synthetic materials has greatly reduced the demand for some raw materials, notably cotton and wool.

Third, the less-developed countries are hostile to private foreign capital because it has colonial overtones. Nor are they willing to remain the suppliers of raw materials. They fear the instability of raw-materials prices and foresee a downward trend. They are inclined to draw back from dependence on the world market. Above all, they identify development with industrialization, and seek to build massive industrial facilities to symbolize their independence and assert their maturity. They could even be following the advice of Alexander Hamilton's *Report on Manufactures:*

> . . . the foreign demand for the products of agricultural countries, is in a great degree, rather casual and occasional, than certain or constant . . . there are natural causes tending to render the external demand for the surplus of agricultural nations a precarious reliance . . .
>
> Considering how fast and how much the progress of new settlements in the United States must increase the surplus produce of the soil . . . there appear strong reasons to regard the foreign demand for that surplus as too uncertain a reliance, and to desire a substitute for it, in an extensive domestic market.
>
> To secure such a market, there is no other expedient, than to promote manufacturing establishments.

THE NETWORK OF WORLD TRADE

The statistics in Table 16 support this pessimistic appraisal. In 1961 world exports totaled $111 billion; they were about one-fifth as large as the American gross national product. But fully half of world exports stayed inside the center of the world economy.[3] The industrial countries imported just $22 billion worth of goods from the periphery, a sum that was merely 20 per cent of world exports and was less than 30 per cent of all imports bought by the industrial countries. Yet this thin trade flow is the one that must transmit the growth impulse from the center countries to the less-developed periphery. Furthermore, this strategic trade flow has grown more slowly than the flow of trade within the industrial center. The dollar value of the trade flow inside the center increased by 100 per cent from 1953 through 1961. But the dollar value of the flow from the periphery grew by only 26 per cent.

In one important case, center-country imports have grown fast, and certain of the less-developed countries have prospered in consequence. The demand for petroleum has pumped great sums of foreign capital into the Near East and Venezuela, and these countries have used their oil revenues to finance their development. Although Venezuela pays large profits to foreign oil companies (almost $400 million in 1960), it can live far beyond its ordinary means. The huge payments surplus of the oil sector ($1.5 billion in 1960) finances a gaping payments deficit in the rest of the economy, paying for imported capital equipment and consumers goods. But the petroleum producers also face trouble. With the discovery of oil in North Africa and Soviet

[3] The "industrial" *versus* "non-industrial" classification used in the table does not exactly match the "developed" *versus* "less-developed" classification. Japan is an industrial country, but by the test of income per person is much less developed than Australia or New Zealand, which are non-industrial countries.

TABLE 16

Trade Between Industrial and Non-industrial Countries in 1961

Trade Flow	Value in Billions of Dollars	Percentage of World Trade *	Percentage Change Since 1953
1. World exports (= world imports) *	111.2	100	+ 63
2. Exports of industrial countries †	80.9	73	+ 82
2a. To industrial countries	56.9	51	+100
2b. To non-industrial countries	24.0	22	+ 51
3. Exports of non-industrial countries	30.3	27	+ 26
3a. To industrial countries	27.5	20	+ 26
3b. To non-industrial countries	7.8	7	+ 24
4. Imports of industrial countries (2a + 3a)	79.4	71	+ 72
5. Imports of non-industrial countries (2b + 3b)	31.8	29	+ 44

* Excludes Soviet-bloc trade.
† North America, Western Europe, and Japan.
Source: General Agreement on Tariffs and Trade, *International Trade*, 1961, pp. 9 and 24.

petroleum sales to non-communist countries, oil prices have weakened. The older producers have had to make room for their new rivals, just as Brazil and Colombia have had to give way before the new coffee-growers of West Africa.

FIG. 16 The change in raw materials prices, 1953 to 1961, selected products and major exporters. The decline in the prices of key raw materials has been reflected in the average export prices of the less-developed countries that export one or two of those raw materials. (Source: International Monetary Fund, *International Financial Statistics*, May, 1962, pp. 32-45.)

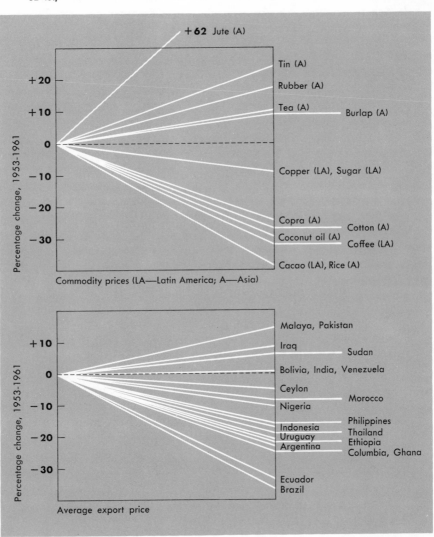

THE PRICES OF PRIMARY PRODUCTS

The recent weakening of oil prices is part of a larger picture. The prices of many primary products have been declining, with coffee and cacao leading the way. This trend, shown in the upper panel of Fig. 16, is reflected in the average export prices of the less-developed countries, shown in the lower panel of the same diagram. As coffee accounts for more than 75 per cent of Colombia's exports, the decline in coffee prices has reduced the average of Colombian export prices by a full 20 per cent. As 35 per cent of Philippine export income derives from coconut oil and another 35 per cent derives from copra, the price decline in these two products has reduced Philippine export prices by 15 per cent.

This apparent downward trend in prices is only half the problem facing the less-developed countries. They must also cope with short-term fluctuations that can be very violent. The years 1955–1961 saw comparative stability in the world economy. There were, of course, two recessions in the United States, but neither one was deep or long, and the European economies suffered no setbacks at all. Yet there were wide short-term swings in raw materials prices. Seven major products showed one or more *year-to-year* price drops greater than 20 per cent: [4]

Cacao	— 27 per cent (1955-56)
Coconut oil	— 26 per cent (1960-61)
Coffee	— 21 per cent (1958-59)
Copper	— 33 per cent (1956-57)
Copra	— 29 per cent (1960-61)
Rubber	— 27 per cent (1960-61)
Wool	— 29 per cent (1957-58)

This short-term instability is nothing new. It was much more pronounced before the Second World War. But the tolerance for price fluctuations is much smaller now. The governments of the less-developed countries are committed to maintain full employment, just like their cousins in North America and Western Europe, although they are not well-equipped to offset serious disturbances such as major price changes. Furthermore, the instability of export prices is usually mirrored in total export earnings. Total receipts can even change by more than prices; when demand declines, price and quantity fall together, and price *times* quantity falls by more than either one alone. Thus, the less-developed countries frequently confront gaping shortages of foreign currency and are obliged to restrict their imports. Some of them have had to curb investment spending, slowing down their planned development.

[4] International Monetary Fund, *International Financial Statistics* (May, 1962), pp. 32-35.

THE FLOW OF PRIVATE CAPITAL

In the nineteenth century there were two large cash flows from center to periphery. Europe's demand for food and raw materials gave rise to one large stream. Europe's lending gave rise to a second. Both of them reflected the center countries' need for raw materials. European capital went to the periphery to expand raw materials production. Some of it was invested directly in mining, plantation agriculture, and ranching. Most of it went into transportation and public utilities, helping to move goods rather than produce them. Thus, fully half the cash that built the American railroads in 1860–1880 came from abroad, mainly from Britain. Between 1860 and 1890, $2.5 billion of foreign capital came to the United States, helping to finance imports of producers goods, including railroad rolling stock.

The less-developed countries of the twentieth century also need foreign funds to finance development. Foreign capital is a claim on foreign resources, and a country that can exercise such a claim is able to invest more than it can save. It can carry on more capital formation than if it were left to its own devices. As a matter of fact, the less-developed countries make more deliberate and systematic use of foreign capital than their predecessors in the nineteenth century. The American companies that borrowed abroad by selling securities in London were not trying to supplement American resources. They did so because it was cheaper and easier to issue securities in London than in New York; the London securities market was better developed and the London dealers were expert in handling new issues. Today, by contrast, governments set out to supplement domestic saving by foreign borrowing. India's Third Five Year Plan, covering 1961–1965, calls for more than $20 billion of new investments—public and private, domestic and foreign. To reach this total, India will need some $6 billion of foreign capital. Hence, the International Bank for Reconstruction and Development (IBRD) has organized a *consortium* of capital-exporting countries. These countries have made commitments to India for the first two years of the Five Year Plan:

Canada	$ 56	million
France	30	"
Germany	364	"
Japan	80	"
United Kingdom	250	"
United States	1,045	"
IBRD and affiliates	400	"
Total	$2,225	"

Some economists believe that the less-developed countries should attract more private foreign capital. They criticize India and other countries for relying so heavily on official funds. The United States, they say, managed to attract private foreign capital—to borrow enormous sums in London and other European financial centers. Why can't India, Egypt, or Brazil? Why can't they attract direct investment from the United States and Western Europe?

Unfortunately there are large barriers to the flow of private capital—and many flaws in the analogy between the less-developed countries of the nineteenth century and those of the twentieth:

1. Most nineteenth-century capital transfers were portfolio investments (bond issues) rather than direct investments (the building of factories and other facilities by foreign companies). If, then, the less-developed countries were to follow the American example, they would borrow foreign money by issuing bonds. Yet the European and American markets for foreign securities have been badly battered in the last 40 years. There were large foreign bond flotations in the 1920's. But with the international financial collapse of the 1930's, this source of capital dried up. Many borrowers suspended interest payments on their bonds; some defaulted on the principal. The New York market for foreign bonds has begun to revive. But investors are still very chary of foreign issues, especially of those that come from the less-developed countries; these countries have chronic payments problems and still maintain exchange controls.

2. Even in the nineteenth century, little foreign capital went into manufacturing. Yet that is where the less-developed countries want it channeled now. Like many European countries, they have placed utilities and transport under public ownership or close regulation. Some Latin-American governments, for example, have clamped low ceilings on the price of electric power to subsidize the power-using industries. They have thereby discouraged foreign investment in new power plants. The trend toward public ownership also threatens early nationalization of the remaining private facilities. And compensation is sometimes inadequate, often delayed. In short, the risks of private investment in power and transport are very large compared to the returns, so that private enterprise in the center countries is not easily persuaded to make new commitments.

3. Because the global demand for raw materials has been so sluggish recently, American companies have not been too anxious to move into mining or plantation agriculture in the less-developed countries. For that matter, some of the less-developed countries are not anxious to attract foreign capital into the extractive industries. They equate extraction with exploitation, and want to reduce their dependence on exports of raw materials.

Despite these barriers and fears, there has been a great deal of foreign investment at the periphery—more than one would forecast knowing all the circumstances. The Organization for Economic Cooperation and Development (OECD) collects and publishes data on the flow of capital to the less-developed countries and to the international organizations that help finance development. The most recent data are summarized in Table 17. The total flow of long-term private capital was smaller than the flow of public money, but did exceed $3.1 billion in 1961; and three-fifths of the private money came from Western Europe, Canada, and Japan, countries that supplied less than half of the total public flow.

Yet the stream of private capital has not grown in the last few years. In fact, the available data suggest a decline in some key components of the total flow, partly because of cuts in new petroleum investment and partly because of political unrest in Latin America.

Policy at the Center

Chapters 3 and 5, discussing commercial and financial policy, emphasized relations among the center countries. Chapter 3, for instance, studied the impact of the European Common Market on the United States, while Chapter 5 examined the monetary problems of the center countries— those that hold the bulk of world reserves. This stress on the center was quite

TABLE 17

Total Flow of Capital to the Less-Developed Countries and to International Organizations Financing Development, 1961 (Millions of dollars)

Type of Capital	United States	Europe, Canada, and Japan	Total
Public Capital			
Grants in aid	1,397	1,373	2,770
Agricultural commodities	1,168	4	1,172
New lending	1,070	961	2,031
less Repayments on old loans *	— 451	— 252	—703
Flow through international organizations	302	553	855
Total official	3,486	2,639	6,125
Private Capital			
Direct investment †	970	1,186	2,156
Other new lending and guaranteed export credits (net)	250	661	911
Flow through international organizations ‡	— 2	110	108
Total private	1,218	1,957	3,175
Grand Total	4,704	4,596	9,300

* After deducting repayments accomplished by new borrowing (refinancing).
† Including reinvested earnings.
‡ Chiefly private purchase of IBRD bonds.
Source: Organization for Economic Cooperation and Development (OECD), *The Flow of Financial Resources to Developing Countries in 1961* (Paris, 1963).

deliberate. For some time to come, international economic trends will be shaped by events within the Atlantic community. If the center prospers, the periphery can prosper; if the center stagnates, the periphery will stagnate. If the center countries can cope with their payments problems, private capital can go where it will earn the highest rewards; if they are plagued by chronic payments problems, money may not venture out or will look for speculative opportunities, rather than long-term profit prospects. If, finally, the center countries grow steadily, their governments will be free to wrestle with the problems of development; if they stagnate or are plagued by instability, their governments will be preoccupied with problems near home and will neglect their responsibilities in the outside world.

Yet the center countries have also to take special notice of the periphery when they formulate their own economic policies. The commercial policies of the center countries can exert a decisive influence on the pattern of development at the periphery. Turned one way, they can draw the less-developed countries into the world economy to capture the full gains from trade; turned the other way, they can force those countries to pull back from foreign trade and cultivate an expensive self-sufficiency. The financial policies of the center countries can influence the pace of development. By encouraging private foreign investment and supplying more official funds, the center can help the periphery to increase capital formation and grow more rapidly. Failing to do so, they may doom the less-developed countries to continued poverty, for population growth threatens to outstrip local capital formation and to keep living standards at their present dismal levels.

COMMERCIAL POLICY

Some of the commercial problems of the less-developed countries cannot be blamed on center-country policies—nor remedied by changes in those policies. The development of synthetic textile fibers like rayon and dacron has held down the demand for cotton and wool. The spread of cotton cultivation has enlarged the supply of natural fibers. These changes in demand and supply have depressed prices and injured the older producers.

But the developed countries have compounded the problems of primary producers. The United States has restricted its lead and zinc imports to protect American miners, injuring Mexico and other major exporters. The United States and Western Europe have restricted their sugar imports, the former to protect its cane-sugar industry, the latter to protect its beet-sugar industry. And European countries have high taxes on several other tropical exports—coffee, tea, and bananas. These are not protective duties, since Europe does not grow these foods; they are merely meant to raise revenue. But these taxes still do damage to the less-developed countries by reducing European consumption. Furthermore, the European Common Market gives preferential treatment to imports from former French and Belgian colonies in Africa, thus discriminating against Latin America and Asia.

The center countries' agricultural policies also aggravate the plight of primary producers. The United States imposes import quotas on wheat, rye, cotton, and other major staples to defend its domestic support prices against import competition. Western Europe uses variable import duties for the very same purpose. Finally, the United States sells its farm surpluses abroad on terms that can hurt other exporters. Under the Food for Peace program, the government sells surplus wheat and other commodities for foreign currencies rather than for dollars, allowing the less-developed countries to increase their food imports without spending their precious foreign-exchange earnings. The program gives enormous aid to many of the less-developed countries, for they have huge food deficits. But these same foreign-currency sales can sometimes displace the exports of other low-income countries instead of supplementing normal consumption.

Over the long run, the center-countries' policies toward manufactured imports will have the strongest impact on the periphery. If the less-developed countries are to grow toward the world economy rather than away from it, they must be encouraged to diversify their exports. Some of them can export a wider range of crops and minerals. Most of them, however, will have to export light manufactured goods—textiles, apparel, ceramics, and the like. A few of these countries are already selling manufactured goods to the center countries, but face high tariffs in the United States and Western Europe. The average U.S. tariff on textile products is as high as 19 per cent (see Table 4); the average tariff on ceramics and glass is 25.8 per cent. What is worse, these trade barriers are apt to rise as the less-developed countries become more competitive. Average wages must reflect average productivity if countries are to balance their foreign transactions. This is why wage rates are so low at the periphery. But in labor-intensive industries like textiles and apparel, output per man-hour does not differ much from country to country; a garment worker at a sewing machine is just about as efficient in Hong Kong or Bombay as in New York or Milan. Hence, the less-developed countries have a distinct cost advantage in labor-intensive production; and when they begin to export manufactures, it is often with stunning effect. They can disrupt established markets in the center countries, forcing workers and communities to make painful adjustments. The center countries are loathe to accept this disruption and have raised new trade barriers, even import quotas, against low-wage textile products. They have promised to lift or liberalize these barriers over the long term, but this pledge may be more often breached than honored.

If the less-developed countries are to participate fully in foreign trade, the United States and Western Europe must welcome imports from the periphery—raw materials and manufactures alike. To this end, as well as to expand its own export trade, the United States will soon begin a new round of tariff bargaining with the European Common Market. It seeks to achieve a better allocation of center-country resources and to provide the less-developed countries with new export markets.

PRICE POLICY AND PRIMARY PRODUCTS

The United States and Western Europe can also aid the low-income countries by trying to stabilize trade in raw materials. The instability of raw-materials prices is expensive to the world as a whole. It propels the periphery toward self-sufficiency. Because they cannot rely on a steady income from primary products, the producing countries seek to reduce their dependence on center-country exports of manufactures.

Past attempts to combat price fluctuations have not been too successful These attempts involved international *commodity agreements* that tried to regulate production, trade, or prices. The sugar agreement imposed export quotas on the producing countries in order to regulate supply. The tin agreement set up a *buffer stock* of tin under the management of the International Tin Council, and instructed the Council to buy and sell tin in order to smooth out prices. The wheat agreement worked on a third principle. The importing countries undertook to buy predetermined quantities of wheat at or above an agreed minimum price, giving exporters an assured minimum income. In return, the exporting countries undertook to sell predetermined quantities at or below an agreed maximum price.

There is now another commodity agreement covering international trade in coffee, and agreements may be written for other primary products. But these commodity agreements are far from perfect. It is difficult to penalize the sugar exporters who exceed their quotas and drive prices down. It is hard to know which price movements should be fought by purchases or sales from a buffer stock. At one point, incidentally, the Tin Council ran out of tin and could not keep the price down. And all these agreements have one major flaw. While working to dampen fluctuations, they also tend to freeze prices, suppressing signals of long-run change in supply or demand. They consequently distort resource allocation, much as the American farm price support program tends to keep too much labor occupied in agriculture. Some observers therefore urge the center countries to try a new approach to stabilization—*compensatory financing* rather than price manipulation.

One simple plan will illustrate this alternative. Suppose that the producing and consuming countries agree to let prices fluctuate in response to changes in supply and demand, but set up a large fund to *indemnify* producers when prices fall. An exporting country would be able to draw on the fund to cover, say, one-half of the short fall in its export earnings caused by a price decline. Suppose Bolivia's tin exports were 50 million pounds. Suppose, further, that the price of tin was $10 per pound this year, but had been $11 last year. Bolivia could draw one-half of ($11 − $10) × 50,000,000, or $25 million, from the indemnity fund. When the price of tin began to rise again, Bolivia would repay its drawings. It might, in fact, repay more than it had drawn if the price rose above the level that prevailed when the agreement came into force.

Payments under such a scheme might not go directly to the producers, but merely to the government of the producing country. Then they would not interfere with resource allocation or give individual producers an incentive to expand output when prices were falling. The compensatory payments would merely serve to smooth out foreign-exchange earnings, allowing the less-developed countries to proceed with their investment plans unhampered by balance-of-payments crises.

FOREIGN AID AND INVESTMENT

If the less-developed countries could count on a stable flow of foreign exchange and a growing market for their manufactured exports, they would have a much better chance to grow. But they would still require long-term foreign capital to exploit their opportunities. The center countries must transfer more resources to the periphery. The United Nations Secretariat has estimated that some $12 billion of foreign capital is needed every year merely to raise per-capita income by 2 per cent annually. This is one-third more than the flow in 1961, described by Table 17.

The center countries may be able to enlarge the flow of private capital. But they are already doing a great deal. For some time, the United States has provided guarantees against the special hazards of foreign investment—expropriation, exchange depreciation, and war damage. Recently, it has begun to offer "all risk" guarantees. A company that plans to build a plant abroad can buy a guarantee from the U.S. government, which would compensate the company if its assets were confiscated, frozen, or destroyed. Several countries grant tax incentives to their investors. The United States, for example, permits an American company to defer its U.S. taxes on income earned abroad, and the president has asked Congress to enact an outright tax credit favoring American firms investing in the less-developed countries. German companies can already take a temporary tax deduction when they make a new investment abroad. Finally, the center countries seek to foster a joint flow of private and official capital. The International Finance Corporation (IFC), a subsidiary of the International Bank for Reconstruction and Development (IBRD), is empowered to invest its funds in new private projects at the periphery; it buys non-voting stock in a new enterprise and claims a share in the profits. It can then sell off its investments when the project gains momentum and private investors are willing to buy its holdings. In effect, the IFC serves a catalytic purpose. By committing its own funds, it seeks to encourage a complementary flow of private capital.

The IBRD or World Bank also seeks to mobilize private capital by selling its own bonds in the developed countries, then making loans to governments and private enterprise in the less-developed countries. It lays special stress on transport and power, but also finances agriculture and industrial development. In 1961 the Bank lent $610 million to 20 countries, including a $90 million loan to Pakistan for agricultural development. In the same year, it borrowed all its money outside the United States, with German investors taking up the largest share of the Bank's new bond issues. But there are limits to the work the World Bank can do. Because it must pay interest on its bonds and redeem them in dollars or other convertible currencies, the Bank must charge 5 per cent or more on its loans to the less-developed countries and must be repaid in "hard" currencies. These terms impose a heavy burden on some borrowers. Their debt-service payments (interest and principal) already absorb too large a part of their export earnings. Brazil, for instance, has had to earmark $13 out of every $100 it earned from exports merely to repay past debts to foreigners. If, then, there is to be an increased flow of funds to the periphery, there must be more foreign aid or long-term, low-interest public lending.

This is discouraging news for many Americans. The United States has been aiding other countries for more than 20 years. It gave Lend-Lease assistance to its allies in the Second World War, then relief to the victors and vanquished alike. The Marshall Plan helped European reconstruction. The Mutual Security Program provided military aid to strengthen the free world against Soviet aggression. Ever since the mid-1960's, moreover, the United States has been lending large sums of money to the less-developed countries through the Export-Import Bank, making other large loans repayable in foreign currencies, and supplying large amounts of surplus food and fiber. Most recently, the Agency for International Development (AID) has begun to make long-term loans repayable in dollars. These bear nominal rates of interest and will not be repaid for 50 years or more. In 1961 United States foreign aid and lending to the less-developed countries totaled almost $3.5 billion, accounting for much more than half the total flow of public funds into the periphery and for more than a third of all long-term capital transfers (see Table 17).

American aid to the less-developed countries has grown in recent years and must continue to grow. But we should not exaggerate the sacrifice involved. In 1961 United States economic aid and long-term lending claimed less than 1 per cent of the gross national product. France, Britain, and other countries were making similar contributions relative to their output, with most of their aid going to former colonies and dependent territories. The

Soviet Union, moreover, has perceived the political advantages of foreign aid. Its commitments are much smaller than those of the United States, but are disbursed to capture the largest tactical advantage. In 1960 Soviet aid totaled $939 million, but a full $802 million went to Egypt, Ghana, Iraq, India, and Indonesia—neutral countries that have a strategic place in Soviet policy.

The United States should not expect immediate gains from its foreign aid. Money does not buy friends or allies. Foreign aid may not even guarantee economic growth. But most authorities agree that the less-developed countries cannot grow without help. And if they do not grow, they may succumb to tyranny.

PROSPECTS

Progress in human affairs sometimes occurs by the slow accretion of small changes in existing institutions and practices, rather than by radical reform. But if the United States and other industrial countries are to meet the challenge posed by the newer nations, they must draw bold plans and commit a larger part of their vast wealth. Nothing we can do will guarantee success. Trade and aid do not assure development, and development does not assure political stability. It may, in fact, usher in drastic change and upheaval in the new nations. But failure to provide opportunities for trade and to furnish large amounts of aid will certainly inhibit growth at the periphery. Stagnation, moreover, will produce frustrations and discontent that will bring a worse sort of disorder. To strengthen the industrial center and knit together center and periphery may be the most important and difficult tasks facing the United States in the second half of the twentieth century.

Allen, William R. and Clark Lee Allen, eds., *Foreign Trade and Finance*. (New York: Macmillan, 1959.) An excellent collection of articles on theory and policy with commentary by the editors.

American Economic Association, *Readings in the Theory of International Trade*. (Philadelphia: Blakiston, 1949.) Includes several classics in trade theory; Chapters 10-17 are especially valuable.

Condliffe, J. B., *The Commerce of Nations*. (New York: W. W. Norton, 1950.) A detailed account of international economic history, stressing the strategic role of Britain in the world economy.

Haberler, Gottfried, *A Survey of International Trade Theory*. (Princeton: International Finance Section, 1961.) An over-all view of modern theory shorn of mathematics and complicated diagrams.

Hallstein, Walter, *United Europe: Challenge and Opportunity*. (Cambridge: Harvard University Press, 1962.) A series of lectures by the President of the EEC Commission explaining the origins, organization, and objectives of the Common Market.

Hicks, J. R., *Essays in World Economics*. (London: Oxford University Press, 1959.) Chapter 3 is a brilliant restatement of the case for free trade.

Holmes, Alan R., *The New York Foreign Exchange Market*. (New York: Federal Reserve Bank of New York, 1959.) A description of the institutions participating in the market, the way trading takes place, and interest arbitrage.

Humphrey, Don D., *The United States and the Common Market*. (New York: Frederick A. Praeger, 1962.) A detailed commentary on U.S. commercial policy under the Trade Agreements Act, with proposals for reform to meet the problems posed by the Common Market.

Meade, James E., *The Balance of Payments*. (London: Oxford University Press, 1951.) The classic treatise on balance-of-payments adjustment under various exchange-rate systems.

Mikesell, Raymond F., ed., *U.S. Private and Government Investment Abroad*. (Eugene: University of Oregon Press, 1962.) A thorough review of American experience as an international investor, with excellent chapters on direct investment, bond issues, and government lending.

Nurkse, Ragnar, *International Currency Experience*. (Geneva: League of Nations, 1944.) A description and critique of international monetary policy during the interwar period, particularly critical of flexible exchange rates.

————, *Equilibrium and Growth in the World Economy*. (Cambridge: Harvard University Press, 1961.) My treatment of "center and periphery" has been strongly influenced by Nurkse's views; see, especially, Chapters 7 and 11.

Ohlin, Bertil, *Interregional and International Trade*. (Cambridge: Harvard University Press, 1933.) The classic statement of the factor-endowments approach to trade theory, with an analysis of factor prices and factor movements.

Robinson, Joan, "The Pure Theory of International Trade," *Review of Economic Studies*, Vol. XIV, No. 2 (1946/47). A superb synthesis of trade theories, with special attention to the role of wages.

Salant, Walter S., and others, *The United States Balance of Payments in 1968*. (Washington: The Brookings Institution, 1963.) A detailed projection of the balance of payments prepared at the request of the President's Council of Economic Advisers, but more interesting for its analytical insight than for its forecasts.

Triffin, Robert, *Gold and the Dollar Crisis*. (New Haven: Yale University Press, 1960.) A controversial interpretation of recent international monetary history, and Professor Triffin's celebrated plan for reform of the IMF.

Tsiang, S. C., "Fluctuating Exchange Rates in Countries with Relatively Stable Economies," *International Monetary Fund Staff Papers,* Vol. VII, No. 2 (October, 1959). An interesting contrast with Nurkse's critical reading of inter-war experience.

United Nations, *International Compensation for Fluctuations in Commodity Trade.* (New York: 1961.) A report by a panel of experts appraising international commodity agreements and proposing a different method for stabilizing trade in raw materials.

United States Congress, Joint Economic Committee, *Factors Affecting the United States Balance of Payments.* (Washington: Government Printing Office, 1963.) A collection of papers by individual experts examining the various components of the balance of payments and proposing remedies for the payments problem.

INDEX

Date Due

DEMCO NO 295

JAN 17 67				